Mississippi Valley Traveler
Quad Cities
Travel Guide

by Dean Klinkenberg

Christy,

Enjoy!

Dean

Words of Thanks

Thanks to Piper and Alex, for their generosity and friendship; to the crew at Blue Cat for their support and encouragement; to Leif for opening the door; to Kopper for his helpful comments on the manuscript; to the good folks at the Quad Cities CVB for their generous help; to the knowledgeable editors at Riverwise Publishing who helped turn a vague idea into a tangible product; and to John for having the patience to allow me to spend weeks on the road, away from home, to indulge my passion for exploring the Mississippi River Valley.

Photo this page: a neon sign for the Black Hawk Shopping Center in Rock Island, Ill. The Sauk leader's name and image are ubiquitous in the Quad Cities.

CONTENTS

INTRODUCING THE QUAD CITIES

Welcome to the Quad Cities, where the Mississippi River flows from east to west—to get from Iowa to Illinois you have to go south! The Quad Cities consist of the Iowa cities of Davenport and Bettendorf and the Illinois cities of Rock Island, Moline, and East Moline. Yes, around here "Quad" actually means five. The Mississippi River cuts through the heart of the region—actually, it is the heart of the region. The cities stretch from the river's banks up and over the bluffs that the Mississippi River excavated thousands of years ago. In the Quad Cities, downtown is literally the part of town that is down the hill.

Each city, remarkably, has maintained a unique personality over the generations: Rock Island is gritty; Davenport is progressive; Moline is conservative; East Moline has strong Hispanic influences; and Bettendorf, well, rich people gotta live somewhere, too. The Mississippi River is the reason that settlers put down their stakes here in the 1830s, and people still flock to its banks to fish, to walk, to gamble, or just to sit and enjoy the view. The Mississippi River unites these disparate cities into a cohesive region.

I've visited the Quad Cities many times in the past two years and consider the region my home away from home. I like the attractions in the Quad Cities, even if they don't totally blow me away. There are plenty of quality ways to pass the time and the people are among the friendliest you will meet anywhere. I know every book says that, but I genuinely mean it. So come on down. Explore the cities. Check out a festival or two. Learn about the region's fascinating history and related stories of American expansion, industrialization, and the shifting economies that continually make and remake cities. Be careful, though. Before you know it, you, too, will consider the Quad Cities your second home.

Don't Miss

• Festivals—you can find one practically any summer weekend, featuring antique motorcycles, very fast go-karts, and music galore (see pages 114-119);

• Listen to the native tunes of the Mississippi River Valley at the River Music Experience (page 62);

• Explore the multitude of attractions on historic Arsenal Island (pages 74-79);

• Hike around moody, post-industrial Sylvan Island (page 97);

• Live the John Deere experience in all its glorious forms (pages 100-103, 109);

• Find the four historic houses with built-in pipe organs!

• Explore the Quad Cities by bicycle (pages 31-32).

Information for Visitors

Tourist information centers are plentiful in the Quad Cities, although hours outside of the summer season

are limited. You can call for information (800.747
.7800/563.322.3911), surf to their web site (www.
visitquadcities.com), or visit one of the four centers.
The place with the most comprehensive information
and hours is the Mississippi Valley Welcome Center
(open daily 8:30–8 from Memorial Day to Labor Day,
otherwise daily 8:30–4:30) located at the Interstate
80/US 67 interchange near LeClaire, Iowa. Other locations include Union Station on the Davenport Riverfront (102 South Harrison St.; M–F 9–5, Sa 10–4
from Memorial Day to Labor Day) and the Moline
Visitor Center (Bass Street Landing, 1601 River Dr.,
Suite 110; M–F 8:30–5; Sa 10–4 from Memorial Day
to Labor Day). New in 2008, the Centennial Bridge
Visitor Center (201 15th St.; 309.277.0937, Th–Sa
10–6, Su 10–4) also has a photo display about the impressive bridge. If you arrive in the area on eastbound
Interstate 80, there is an Illinois Welcome Center just
after the exit for Illinois Highway 84 (800.452.4368;
daily 8–6:30 from Memorial Day to Labor Day; daily
8–4:30 the rest of the year) that has information on
the Quad Cities plus a decent overlook of the Mississippi Valley.

The Quad Cities are located in the Central Time
Zone, the same as Chicago.

Like any metropolitan area, crime happens in the
Quad Cities, and visitors need to take sensible precau-
tions. For example, don't leave valuables visible inside
your car; lock them in the trunk or take them with
you. Generally speaking, though, don't work yourself
into a tizzy worrying about crime.

About This Book

This is a travel guide, in case you haven't noticed. But,
unlike many travel guides, this one includes more of
the author, me, in the text. Yes, I want you to know

about all the terrific attractions in the Quad Cities, but I also want you to know some of the back story, like why certain places excite me.

I have a touch of attitude when it comes to travel. I want to get away from the familiar. I am not a fan of chain stores, malls, mass consumption, or mass marketing. If all you want to do on vacation is lie on the beach, sip apple-tinis, and shop at Eddie Bauer; if you buy all your art at the Pottery Barn; if your idea of a nice meal is the grilled chicken platter at TGI Fridays, then this book may not be for you. Sure, you can find national brands anywhere in the Quad Cities—if that's what you need—but why not take a chance and try something that hasn't been focus grouped and mass marketed to the lowest common denominator? Why not chill out listening to tunes at the River Music Experience or Redstone Room? Why not sample some local flavor with a hand-crafted beer and comfort food at the Blue Cat Brew Pub? Why not treat yourself to the homey atmosphere of a bed-and-breakfast? Relax, slow down, hang out, talk to people. That's my prescription for enjoying travel anywhere, and it will be very rewarding in the Quad Cities, too.

✔ TIP: If you want to know more about my experiences writing this book, visit my web site (www.mississippivalleytraveler.com). I'll also be posting articles about Mississippi River towns that wouldn't fit in this volume.

About My Picks

This book has no advertisements, paid or otherwise. No one paid for a spot in the book. No one gave me a free meal or free place to stay in exchange for a listing. The only freebie I got in the course of researching this book was a ticket to the Celtic Highland Games of the Quad Cities. The recommendations in this book, for better or for worse, are based upon my judgment of what is good, interesting, fascinating, or just worthy of your time.

Restaurants

Look, I can't possibly eat at every single restaurant that might be good. I don't have time for it; I can't afford it; and I don't want to look like the Stay Puft Marshmallow Man, again. That's just the way it goes. Restaurants get on my radar screen through recommendations from locals and visitors. I also pay attention to the places that are always busy. If a restaurant is packed and locals speak highly of it, I'll put it in the book, even if I don't get a chance to taste their food personally. For each restaurant in this book, however, at the very least, I visit to check out the visuals and to look over a menu.

Bars

My preferences tend toward dives and brewpubs, which are both over-represented in this book. The region has three outstanding brewpubs, each serving up distinctive flavors in brews, food, and atmosphere. There are also dozens if not hundreds of friendly neighborhood taverns. Let me know your favorites. Maybe we'll meet there for a drink, especially if you're buying.

Accommodations

I have included a wide range of accommodation options, from campgrounds to bed-and-breakfasts to luxury hotels. My bias is to support independent motels, inns, and bed-and-breakfasts. I only provide detailed information for chain hotels that have a property directly on the River Road. Otherwise, I simply note where the chain hotels are located—after all, they tend to cluster like politicians around fundraisers. A note about the rates cited in the book: I asked for rates

Celtic Games Hammerthrow

for two adults on a Saturday night during the summer, which is peak season. In most cases, rates were quoted by staff directly, but in some cases I used online search engines to generate estimates. So here's the disclaimer: hotel rates can vary tremendously depending upon a number of factors that are beyond my control. You may be able to do better than the rates quoted here, especially during the week, but many of the smaller places—bed-and-breakfast inns and mom-and-pop motels—have little room to bargain, unless you want to negotiate an extended stay. Also, I assume you know that budget motels are a mixed bag. Some are noisy; rooms are not always of consistent quality; and sometimes they get bad reputations, although often for reasons that are greatly exaggerated. But, they usually have the most affordable rates. If all you want is a cheap place to sleep, budget motels should suit you fine. If a little dirt and a few truck drivers scare you, however, you should probably stay somewhere else. So there, you've been warned.

HISTORY

The earliest inhabitants migrated into this region about 12,000 years ago, on the tail of their primary food sources—mastodon and mammoth. Anthropologists labeled this group "Big Game Hunters." When mastodon and mammoth became extinct about 10,000 years ago, the Big Game Hunters settled into small communities of hunters and gatherers, so anthropologists called them Small Communities of Hunters and Gatherers. (Just kidding.) The area was blessed with an abundance of natural resources and these small communities flourished, reaching their cultural peak between 500 BCE and 1000 CE (the Woodland Period). Remarkably, these communities had extensive trade routes with cultures as far west as the Rocky Mountains and possibly deep into South America, with the Mississippi River serving as a key transport route.

Sauk and Mesquakie Move In

By the 16th century, Native Americans were organized around two major language groups: 1) Algonquin, spoken by the Illiniwek who lived between the Mississippi, Illinois and Wisconsin Rivers and Lake Michigan; and 2) Siouan, who lived west of the Mississippi. Less than 100 years later, nearly all of these groups had been replaced by the Sauk and Mesquakie.

These closely related nations consisted of Algonquin speakers who had roots in northeast Canada. Both nations lived in settled villages and intermarriage was common. The Mesquakie developed a reputation for being quick to pick quarrels with their Indian neighbors, which led to the nickname outagami for their perceived cunning and cruelty. French explorers translated this word as renard, which gave us the English name for the Mesquakie—Fox—a name that the Mesquakie did not find flattering.

Both groups were forced to migrate west for many reasons, including a need to find new hunting grounds, land pressure from advancing European settlements, and retreat from the Iroquois, against whom they had lost a series of battles. The Sauk had a relatively peaceful migration, eventually settling along the Rock River where they built a village called Sauke-nuk (in present day Rock Island, Illinois).

In contrast, the Mesquakie journey west was catastrophic. At one time, they controlled a number of rivers used by French fur traders and used their leverage to extort goods from traders in exchange for safe passage. The French eventually tired of this and decided to solve their problem by exterminating the Mesquakie. The Mesquakie fled, naturally. After months on the move, they paused at a crude fort near Starved Rock in north-central Illinois. Their presence was soon detected, and they were surrounded by French and allied troops. On September 8, 1730, they tried to escape but were spotted. The resulting attack killed over 1,000 men, women and children—nearly the entire nation. Those who escaped sought shelter with the Sauk along the Rock River.

The Mesquakie never really recovered from their near annihilation. They remained poor and lacked the resources to move to winter hunting grounds. Many ended up working in lead mines around Dubuque, mines that supplied European settlers and that would eventually entice more European settlers into the area.

Europeans Find a Big River

In 1541, *Hernando de Soto* became the first European to see the Mississippi River. His discovery, however, failed to generate much excitement back home. In fact, there was no additional exploration by Europeans until *Louis Joliet* and *Father James Marquette* reached the Mississippi River on June 17, 1673—over a century later. Although Joliet and Marquette made no territorial claims, they were soon followed by plenty of people who did: representatives of the French, Spanish, and British crowns soon planted the flags of their respective nations along the Mississippi River. Native Americans were pulled into the inevitable conflicts, often fighting each other on behalf of or beside the colonial powers.

Although the French explored much of the Upper Mississippi Valley before any other Europeans, military defeats in the 1760s forced France to cede control of its territory west of the Mississippi to Spain and its lands east of the Mississippi to England. A few years later, the North American political landscape changed again with that American Revolution thing that kicked off in 1776. During negotiations to end the American Revolution, the British insisted that their Indian allies be allowed to live in their traditional lands; the Americans agreed, reluctantly. The Treaty, however, did not ultimately grant long-term security to the Sauk and Mesquakie. When the territory was controlled by the British, the Indians made annual trips to Fort Malden in Canada where they received supplies and gifts. After the Treaty of Paris, these trips continued, as did British gift-giving and bad-mouthing of the Americans. This did not go over very well with the Americans and would eventually be a factor in the demise of the Sauk and Mesquakie.

American Expansion

With the Louisiana Purchase in 1803, the territory around the Quad Cities was united under the U.S. flag. Whites entering the region after the Louisiana

Purchase, unlike previous generations of Europeans, were intent on creating permanent settlements and taking ownership of land. Land disputes erupted and were often exacerbated when American officials negotiated land treaties with representatives of Indian nations who were not empowered to sign treaties.

In November 1804, for example, four Sauk Indians traveled to St. Louis to ease tensions after some of their comrades had killed white settlers. *William Henry Harrison*, Governor of the Indiana Territory and a future President of the United States, took advantage of the situation to negotiate a treaty with the group. The resulting

Fort Armstrong (courtesy of Rock Island County Historical Society)

document ceded 15,000,000 acres of Sauk and Mesquakie lands to the United States for $2,234.50 down and $1,000 annually. Never mind that none of the Indians had the legal authority to negotiate a treaty, this document would form the foundation for all future legal disputes between the Sauk and Mesquakie Indians and the U.S. government.

In the early 19th century, continuing disputes with Great Britain held back American westward expansion. In spite of the Treaty of Paris, the Brits maintained trading relationships with Indians in the Upper Midwest and actively encouraged them to resist American rule. When hostilities between Great Britain and the United States were renewed with the War of 1812, many Sauk and Mesquakie relocated deep in the Missouri Territory. Their leader, *Keokuk*, believed that resisting the Americans was a losing proposition. The Sauk who remained behind at Saukenuk looked for leadership from a man called *Makataimeshekiakiak* or *Black Hawk*.

Black Hawk (courtesy of Davenport Public Library)

Again caught in the middle, the Sauk under Black Hawk's leadership eventually sided with the Brits but were not involved in any fighting until July 19, 1814, when Black Hawk and his warriors ambushed a group of supply boats commanded by *Lieutenant John Campbell*. Sixteen Americans died in the attack. The island where Campbell's boat ran aground is now part of East Moline and bears his name.

After signing the Treaty of Ghent to end the War of 1812, the U.S. government negotiated separate treaties with the Indian nations that fought with the British. The Sauk were among the last to settle. In their treaty, they were forced to accept a paragraph that re-affirmed the terms of the 1804 treaty, language that ceded their lands east of the Mississippi River. Black Hawk later swore that he and other Sauk leaders were unaware of that paragraph. Emboldened by the end of the war, *President Madison* began a major offensive to move the Indians out of all territories east of the Mississippi, so white settlers could move in.

European Settlers Arrive

In May 1816, the 8th U.S. Infantry, commanded by *General Thomas Smith*, arrived in Rock Island and started building a fort that Smith named after General John Armstrong. The location chosen for the fort was supposed to be off-limits under the 1804 treaty, but building progressed anyway. General Smith invited the neighboring Indians to the fort for a chat, who, after resisting initially, attended and agreed not to kill any soldiers. Other early residents included *George Davenport* and his family. Davenport, a native of England and an American veteran of the War of 1812, came to establish a commissary to serve the soldiers. His neighbor across the river was *Antoine LeClaire*, who worked as an interpreter and Indian agent for Fort Armstrong. Both Davenport and LeClaire had warm relationships with their Indian neighbors.

Illinois achieved statehood in 1818 but most of the population growth was concentrated in the southern and eastern portions of the state. Western Illinois had large Indian populations along the Mississippi River but few white settlers. On May 10, 1823, development in western Illinois got a big boost when Fort Armstrong hosted *The Virginia*, the first steam-powered boat to reach the Rock Island Rapids. With the opening of a quicker mode of transportation, large numbers of settlers poured into the area, many of whom would settle illegally on Indian lands.

The Black Hawk War

In the late 1820s, encroachments on Indian lands grew more frequent. Two distinct philosophies about how to respond emerged in the Sauk and Mesquakie nations. One group believed they could not reasonably resist American force and should accept the terms of relocation to lands west of the Mississippi. This group was led by Keokuk. The other group believed that existing treaties were not valid because they had not been negotiated by Sauks with the proper authority. This group was led by Black Hawk, who was growing increasingly agitated at the treaty violations.

Under threat from federal forces, Keokuk and his followers left Saukenuk in 1829 and settled west of the Mississippi. Black Hawk, however, continued to return to Saukenuk from winter grounds for the next two years. When he returned to Saukenuk in 1831, he found squatters living in the lodges at Saukenuk. Black Hawk's return sparked several small skirmishes and renewed threats from the Illinois governor to exterminate the Indians if the federal government failed to remove them permanently. Weakened by the departure of many Sauk and Mesquakie families, Black Hawk sought alliances with nearby Kickapoos, Potawatomis, and Ho-Chunk (Winnebago).

Among those who offered support was *White Cloud*, a prominent leader of Ho-Chunk communities along the Rock River. By June of 1831, however, large numbers of federal troops had moved into the area, prompting Black Hawk to return to the west bank of the Mississippi. Soon after that, the army moved into Saukenuk and torched it. Rebuked, Black Hawk signed a new treaty promising to stay on the western side of the Mississippi River, to forego any future visits to British forts, and to recognize Keokuk as the legitimate leader of the Sauk.

Tensions between the Indians and settlers never really abated, however. White settlers regularly ambushed Indians and desecrated their grave sites. Meanwhile, the federal government failed to supply the corn it promised under the terms of the treaty. Faced with starvation, some Indians returned to their ancestral lands in Illinois to harvest any remaining corn, but this move only exacerbated tensions with whites.

In the middle of this mess, Black Hawk accepted an offer from White Cloud to relocate to a Ho-Chunk village along the Rock River in north-central Illinois, breaking his agreement with the U.S. government. Encouraged by rumors that the British would offer support, Black Hawk crossed the Mississippi in April 1832 with 800 Sauk and Mesquakie and 200 Ho-Chunk, intent on re-establishing the Sauk in ancestral lands and proving the injustice of American claims. Black Hawk's actions did not go unnoticed; Illinois rapidly organized several hundred volunteers to pursue him.

Very quickly Black Hawk realized that no help was coming from the British. Further, in spite of White Cloud's assurances, the Ho-Chunk, fearing reprisals from state and federal officials, did not want the Sauks living in their village. Black Hawk moved northwest and, after the Potawatomis also refused to help him, was ready to give up and return to the west side of the Mississippi. Hopes for a peaceful settlement ended when a group of Illinois militia botched a surrender attempt by Black Hawk and triggered a brief fight known as the Battle of Stillman's Run. Although few people were killed in the battle, any hopes for a quick, peaceful settlement ended, and Black Hawk gave up his plan to return to the west via the Rock River. Illinois mustered an additional 2,000 men, including a young *Abraham Lincoln* leading a company of volunteers from Sangamon County, Illinois.

The ensuing war was more of a lengthy game of hide-and-seek, with Black Hawk and his followers on the run most of the time, trying to stay ahead of a motley group of undisciplined volunteers. Black Hawk made at least two additional attempts to surrender, both of which were misinterpreted by the militias and led to more battles and continued retreat. The Sauk moved through northwestern Illinois and into southern Wisconsin before making a break for the Mississippi River at Bad Axe (north of Prairie du Chien).

The only major battle of the war occurred on August 2 when the pursuing troops finally caught up with the majority of the Sauk force. Black Hawk and White Cloud tried to convince the group to continue north toward Ho-Chunk villages and a possible safe haven, but most of the remaining band wanted to get across the Mississippi as quickly as possible. Black Hawk, White Cloud, and a few others separated from the main group and went north, while the majority built rafts to cross the river. Unfortunately, the pursuing armies converged on the main group before most could safely cross the river.

Initially, both sides fought in equal numbers, but federal troops and volunteers flooded into the battle and turned it into a rout, killing more than 200 Sauk men and women. Meanwhile, 150 Sauk had managed to cross the Mississippi safely into Iowa but were immediately detected by Wabasha, a Sioux chief who was aiding the Americans. Most of these Sauk were tracked and killed by the Sioux. Of the 1,000 Sauk who had followed Black Hawk across the Mississippi River back into Illinois, fewer than 200 survived.

Black Hawk was eventually convinced to give up—again—so he surrendered to the Ho-Chunk agent at Fort Crawford (Prairie du Chien). In the aftermath of the war, many Indians—even those who had been friendly and cooperated with the United States—were forced by the American government to make additional land concessions. Black Hawk and White Cloud were escorted by *Jefferson Davis*, the future President of the Confederate States of America, to a prison camp at Jefferson Barracks in St. Louis (see side story, page 19).

Black Hawk After the War

Black Hawk and his partners, White Cloud and Napope, served about seven months in prison at Jefferson Barracks in St. Louis. While imprisoned, their visitors included the author Washington Irving and the painter George Catlin. In April 1833, Black Hawk was sent to the east coast, where he was supposed to spend additional time in prison at Fort Monroe in Virginia. Prior to arriving at the fort, they stopped in Washington where he met President Jackson and other government officials. The Indians served only a few weeks at Fort Monroe, during which time they posed for more portraits. After their release, they were escorted home on a route that passed through several cities, an attempt by the U.S. government to impress upon the Indians the might of American power. It worked. Black Hawk was formally released in October 1833 into the custody of Keokuk, and, other than a few token attempts to challenge Keokuk's leadership, Black Hawk kept a low profile. He died on October 3, 1838, and was buried in a log tomb in a sitting position. In July 1839, the grave was raided and his remains stolen. Black Hawk's sons pled with the governor of the Iowa Territory for help, who succeeded in regaining possession. The governor had them moved to the Burlington Geological and Historical Society in Burlington, Iowa, where they remained hidden away from the public for several years, until, perhaps in an act of divine retribution, the museum burned to the ground in 1855, destroying Black Hawk's bones in the process.

For all the troubles Black Hawk and Keokuk endured, Keokuk got a town in Iowa named after him, while Black Hawk's name became ubiquitous, appearing on bridges, towns, counties, hotels, a college, a professional hockey team, even a shopping mall in Rock Island located near the former location of Saukenuk.

Antoine LeClaire (from *Davenport, Past and Present*, by F.B.Wilkie)

With the war over and Indians removed to the West, development took off in the area and waves of settlers poured in. The area around the confluence of the Rock River and the Mississippi River would grow quickly into an important transportation and manufacturing center.

The Cities Emerge

It's hard to imagine anyone who left bigger footprints in the Quad Cities, both literally and figuratively, than *Antoine LeClaire*. Born on the Michigan frontier to a French Canadian father and a Potawatomi mother, LeClaire was a gifted polyglot. He spoke French, Spanish, English, and at least a dozen Indian languages and put those skills to good use as a professional translator. The most valuable compensation he received was land — gifts from the Indians he befriended, eventually owning enormous expanses of real estate in the areas that would later become the cities of Davenport, Moline, and LeClaire. His girth grew with his wealth, as he was reputed to weigh upwards of 350 pounds in his later years.

One of LeClaire's close friends was *Colonel George Davenport*, who made a good living operating a commissary for Fort Armstrong, then diversified his portfolio by entering the fur trade. The men became friends through their work at Fort Armstrong. LeClaire and Davenport built homes within sight of each other, albeit on opposite sides of the river—the Colonel building his on Arsenal Island and LeClaire on the bluffs across the river.

LeClaire owned a lot of land but lacked the money to develop it. To kick-start the new town of Davenport, LeClaire sold several parcels to developers in 1836. LeClaire named the

LeClaire house in Davenport

town to honor his friend after efforts to put Davenport's name to the town across the river failed. The area where Davenport lived became known as Rock Island, while the area where LeClaire lived became Davenport, although the Colonel never lived there. LeClaire's name is attached to a river town a bit further northeast, even though Antoine lived in what is now Davenport, never in LeClaire. Confused? We'll just move on.

Many other people tried to push development in the region, as well. More than 20 towns sprang up along the Mississippi River in the first seven years after Black Hawk's surrender, and many of them disappeared as quickly as they were planned.

In one case, a group of investors platted Rock Island City on the site of Saukenuk, purchasing 600 acres from George Davenport for the city. Founders had big plans for the town and solicited investors from around the U.S., including from the well-known attorney and U.S. Senator, *Daniel Webster*. The financial panic of 1837 killed the town's prospects and the investors lost their money; Webster lost $60,000.

In spite of the failures of many early communities,

the core cities—Davenport, Rock Island, and Moline—took root and grew into important population centers. Steamboat traffic fueled trade and the presence of the dangerous rapids ensured that the Tri-Cities would serve a vital role in the transportation network.

Railroads built routes to the Tri-Cities, adding to the economic momentum and vaulting the Tri-Cities into the role of regional commercial hub. Settlers arrived from the south and the east—Germans, then Swedes, Belgians, Irish, and Greeks—pumping additional life into the region.

Colonel George Davenport (from *Davenport, Past and Present*, by F.B.Wilkie)

As the Civil War loomed, residents of the Tri-Cities had divided loyalties. The liberal Germans of Davenport and the New Englanders in Moline were fervent abolitionists, while residents of Rock Island, many of whom had Southern roots, favored legal slavery. In spite of these sentiments, however, when war broke out, most residents of Rock Island were against secession and refused to support the Confederacy. Large numbers of men from the area volunteered for the Union Army. Camp McClellan was established in Davenport and became a major processing point for Iowa Volunteers.

After the Civil War, the sawmill industry boomed. Huge log rafts, some nearly a half-mile long, floated down the Mississippi from the pine forests of Minnesota and Wisconsin. The Rock Island-based Mead, Smith, and Mersh opened a sawmill in nearby Coal Valley and hired young *Frederick Weyerhaeuser* as manager. When the mill in Rock Island went under, Weyerhaeuser and his brother-in-law, *Frederick Denkmann*, bought it for $3,000, with just $500 down. The sawmill succeeded and Weyerhaeuser and Denkmann became a dominant force in the industry.

Weyerhaeuser moved to Minnesota in 1896, then to the Pacific Northwest as the forests of the North became depleted and the industry lumbered to the

Davenport House on Arsenal Island

west coast. The Weyerhaeuser mill in Rock Island closed in 1905, but a few sawmills stayed open until 1970.

Even though the sawmills faded away, the Tri-Cities remained a vibrant manufacturing center and the communities benefited from the growing farm economy in Iowa and Illinois. The John Deere Company employed thousands of workers, as did other farm implement manufacturers. The downtown areas became retail centers. Universities such as Augustana College began offering classes. By 1900, the Tri-Cities region was a bustling regional hub with a total population near 100,000.

20th Century Growth

After rapid growth through the middle and end of the 19th century, the older Tri-Cities were joined by a couple of upstarts. The *Bettendorf brothers* built a huge manufacturing plant in the town of Gilbert, which promptly voted to rename itself in honor of the industrial pioneers. Across the river, *E.H. Guyer*'s dream of turning a swamp into a thriving new city began to take shape when his city incorporated in 1902 as East Moline. Both cities attracted new industries and immigrants, including a substantial number of workers recruited from Mexico to fill labor shortages during World War I.

World War II sent the Quad Cities' manufacturing industry into overtime. The federal government purchased the old Bettendorf factory and used it to build tanks. Employment at the Rock Island Arsenal grew from nearly 3,000 in 1939 to 19,000. Many of the new employees were blacks from the South who had been recruited by the Arsenal. The flood of new workers faced a housing shortage, in part because blacks were excluded from most neighborhoods, so the federal government built 300 apartments in Rock Island's west end. After the war ended, jobs at the Arsenal were slashed and many blacks, shut out from many other occupations by discrimination, were unable to find new employment in the area. With high rates of unemployment and poverty, life at the Arsenal Courts quickly turned sour.

The years immediately after World War II were often chaotic. Incomes dropped as overtime work dried up; returning soldiers displaced women and minorities who had been hired to work during the war; labor and management conflict that had been held in check during the war exploded into the open; labor unions fought each other for the right to represent workers.

Labor unrest peaked in 1950 when 14,000 workers were on strike in the Quad Cities. In spite of these troubles, the Quad Cities, like much of the United States, enjoyed economic growth. Each city annexed land and new housing subdivisions popped up seemingly overnight.

Gambling, which had been a part of the QC culture since at least the Civil War, also was booming. A series of crackdowns, instigated primarily through the efforts of a single moral do-gooder, *Marie Van Muelbrock*, and a sympathetic state's attorney, finally ended the practice in 1951, at least until 1991 when gambling on riverboats was legalized. Signs of big changes were afoot, however. With the growth of shopping malls and suburban housing developments in the 1960s and 1970s, retail stores closed in the older neighborhoods and the downtown areas began to resemble ghost towns.

The Depressing '80s

The 1980s were tough. The area suffered a series of devastating job losses as major employers shuttered factories or went out of business: the Rock Island Railroad went under in 1980, eliminating 7,000 jobs; the IH/Case Farmall plant in Rock Island closed in 1986 and the IH/Case plant in Bettendorf followed in 1987; Caterpillar closed its Bettendorf plant in 1986 and its Davenport facility in 1987; even stalwart John Deere made deep cuts in its workforce.

The QC today has rebounded. After hemorrhaging thousands of jobs in the 1980s, the QC economy diversified into the health care and service sectors. The community refocused back on the river. Riverboat gambling arrived in the early 1990s. New parks and trails were built along the river. The arts scene is growing. People are returning to the downtown areas, some to live, some to work, and many to play along the river.

GREAT RIVER ROAD ROUTE OVERVIEW

For my purposes, the boundaries of the Quad Cities are formed by Interstate 80 in the north and east and Interstate 280 in the south and west. Sorry, LeClaire and Muscatine. The Great River Road goes through the heart of the Quad Cities.

On the Iowa side, it follows:

- U.S. Highway 67,
- U.S. Highway 61, and
- Iowa Highway 22;

On the Illinois side, the Great River Road follows, more or less:

- Illinois Highway 92,
- River Drive in Moline, and
- Illinois Highway 84.

River Crossings

There are five bridges across the Mississippi River in the Quad Cities:

• The Fred Schwengel Memorial Bridge is a functional, uninspired bridge; completed in 1966, it carries Interstate 80 across the river.

• The twin suspension bridges of the Iowa-Illinois Memorial Bridge for I-74 connecting Moline, Ill., with Bettendorf, Iowa. The northbound span was built in 1935 by the Works Progress Administration and the southbound span was added in 1960. Both will probably be replaced in the next decade.

• The historic Government Bridge (aka the Arsenal

Interstate 280 Bridge

Bridge) that connects LeClaire Street in Davenport, Iowa, to 1st Avenue and 24th Street in Rock Island, Ill. The Government Bridge was completed in 1896 on the piers of the 1872 bridge. It is a steel truss design with a unique swing span that can rotate 360° to allow river traffic to pass.

• The Rock Island Centennial Bridge for US Highway 67 connects Gaines Street in Davenport, Iowa, to 15th Street in Rock Island, Ill. Completed in 1940 and paid for entirely by the city of Rock Island, the Centennial Bridge is a graceful execution of a steel arch design. It was the first four lane bridge across the Mississippi River.

• The Interstate 280 Bridge, completed in 1970, is a sharp contrast to the area's other interstate bridge, with a graceful steel arch supporting the road deck. I bet Fred Schwengel wished this bridge carried his name.

Streets and Avenues

Most every city here uses numbered streets and avenues, which means if you follow 15th Street when you really want 15th Avenue, you may end up in the Mississippi River instead of that brewpub you want to check out. It also means that when you are asking about an address, you need to know which city it is in. Asking for 14th Street isn't good enough. You need to know that the 14th Street you want is the one in Davenport, not the one in Moline. If that's not confusing enough, you may notice that streets go perpendicular to the river, except in Davenport where they parallel the river. In most cases, perpendicular to the river means north-south, except for Hampton, where perpendicular to the river is nearly east-west, which is the direction streets in Davenport go, even though they parallel the river. I'm sure that clears up the confusion. Maybe this will simplify things. If you are like me and you use the river as a landmark to help navigate around town, remember that the Mississippi flows from east to west through the heart of the Quad Cities, so when you are driving parallel to the river, you are therefore going east or west. It takes some getting used to. I've been turned around many times.

Getting To and Out of Dodge

I bet you arrived here by car, probably on one of the major Interstates that cross through the area: 80, 88, 74, or 280. If you came on the Iowa Great River Road, you arrived either on US Highway 67 from the north or Iowa Highway 22 from the south. On the Illinois side, the Great River Road from the north is Illinois Highway 84; from the south, it is Illinois Highway 92. If you stay on any of the Great River Road routes, you will pass through the heart of the Quad Cities. If you arrive via Interstate Highway, you will fly right past the fun unless you exit onto one of these routes.

Quad City International Airport, founded as Moline Airport, began regular commercial service in

1926. It is on the southern edge of Moline, near the intersection of Interstates 280 and 74. It is served by five airlines: AirTran Airways, American Eagle, Delta Connection, Northwest Airlink, and United Express. Access to downtown Moline from the airport is quick, about ten minutes, by taking I-74 westbound. A taxi will cost you $10–$20 to downtown Moline, $20–$30 to downtown Rock Island, and $25–$35 to downtown Davenport or the hotels in Bettendorf. You may have to call for a taxi, as there is not always a queue at the QC Airport. Rates and phone numbers are posted by exit 7, near baggage claim. You can also take a Metro-LINK bus (Route 20) for $0.80 from the airport to downtown Moline.

In Davenport, the **Charles J. Wright Transit Center** (304 W. River Dr.; 563.326.5127; daily 9–9) is the bus terminal for Greyhound and Burlington Trailways, as well as the local CitiBus. National buses have daily departures to the Iowa cities of Burlington, Cedar Rapids, and Des Moines, plus departures to Omaha, Chicago, and Indianapolis. In Moline, the bus terminal is at **Centre Station** (1200 River Dr.; 309.764.4257; M–F 6:15a–7p, Sa 8:15a–5p, Su 9:15a–4:30p); busses from here have daily departures to Chicago, Des Moines, and Indianapolis. Specific departure times vary from day to day and change frequently. Call the bus lines or check the Internet for current schedules (Greyhound: 563.326.5127; www. greyhound.com. Burlington Trailways: 563.322.1876; www.burlingtontrailways.com).

Honestly, though, if you're going to be exploring the territory along the River Road, you are better off just

For more information and updates, visit my web site at www.mississippivalleytraveler.com.

renting a car. Bus routes to river towns north of the Quad Cities are ridiculously time consuming, although you may have slightly better luck going south. If you want to rent a car, you can go to the airport, where several national chains have offices (Avis, Budget, Enterprise, Hertz, and National/Alamo). In addition, Avis (800.527.0700), Enterprise (800.736.8222), and Hertz (800.654.3131) have other locations around the Quad Cities; call their reservation lines for details.

The nearest Amtrak station is in Galesburg, Ill., about 45 miles south. From Galesburg, you must take a bus to reach the Quad Cities.

Getting Around

Driving is a piece of cake. Just pay attention to those pesky numbered streets and avenues. (See page 27).

Be aware that many intersections in the area, especially in Davenport, use surveillance cameras; don't run red lights. A few places also use cameras to monitor speed; you may get a ticket if you are driving too fast. One last note: the police in Rock Island are vigilant in their pursuit of thoughtless drivers who don't use their turn signals properly. If you fail to signal a turn or turn your blinker on at the last minute, you may get a personal interaction with a member of the Rock Island Police, like I did. Don't say I didn't warn you.

Local busses can get you around town fairly well, but you may have a bit of a wait for some connections. Operating hours are very limited, however, especially at night and on weekends. It's a good idea to call ahead to confirm times and schedules. The bus systems are: **Bettendorf Transit** (563.344.4085/563.386.1350; fare = $0.60; operating hours M–F 6a–6p, Sa 8:30–5:30), Davenport (**CitiBus**; 563.888.2151; fare=$1; operating hours M–F 6a–6:30p, Sa 9a–6:30p), and the Illinois federation called **MetroLINK** (309.788.3360;

fare = $0.80; M–F 5:30a–9p, Sa 7:30a–5:30p, Su
8a–4:30p but no bus service on major holidays). Trans-
fers within the same system are usually free, but trans-
ferring busses between may cost a bit extra. You can
transfer between MetroLINK and Bettendorf busses
at the Centre Station in Moline and between Metro-
LINK ($0.30) and CitiBus in Rock Island's Ground
Transportation Center or in The District ($0.10).

Between Memorial Day and Labor Day you can zip
between cities on both sides of the river on the **Channel Cat Water Taxis** (800.297.0037/309.788.3360;
M,Tu 11a–7:40p, W,Th 11a–7:50p, F,Sa,Su 9a–7:15p,
weekends only in September), which operate above
Lock and Dam 15. Catch a ride at one of the following stops: 1) Moline Landing (Celebration Belle
pier), 2) Isle of Capri in Bettendorf, 3) Village of East
Davenport, and 4) John Deere Commons in Moline.
On Wednesday and Thursday there is an additional
stop at The Quarter in East Moline. A $6 ticket buys
you unlimited rides for a single day; pay as you board.
You can bring your bike on the boat as long as it is not
too crowded.

It is easy to explore the area by bicycle, although the
hills can make for a challenging ride. The bike paths
along the river are generally flat and take you past a
good cross-section of the communities. Most other attractions are within a short distance of the downtowns,
but be prepared to scale the previously mentioned
hills along the way. Between April and September,
bicycles can be rented for $7/hour or $28/day at the
Visitors' Centers at Davenport's Union Station (M–F
8:30–4:30, Sa,Su 10–4 from June to September),
Moline Centre (M–F 8:30–4:30, Sa 10–4 from June
to September), or at the **Centennial Bridge Visitor Center** (Th–Sa 10–6, Su 10–4). There are many
paved bike/pedestrian paths in the Quad Cities. On

the Iowa side, the **Davenport Riverfront Trail** parallels the Mississippi River from Credit Island Park to Bettendorf where it ends at the Isle of Capri Casino. The **Duck Creek Recreational Trail** is another exceptional trail that runs 12 miles through the heart of area from Davenport's Emeis Park to Bettendorf's Duck Creek Park. On the Illinois side, the **Mississippi River Trail** begins in Sunset Park and goes 65 miles to Savanna, Illinois, passing through Moline and East Moline along the way.

Reliable taxi providers include Crosstown Cab (563.381.1000/309.762.6500) and Max's Cab Company (563.324.9000/309.788.4100); both serve the entire Quad Cities area. Call to arrange a ride.

Holding up the Twin Bridges

Bix Biederbeck Inn, Davenport, Iowa

BETTENDORF
B1. Pigeon Creek Park
B2. Eagle's Landing Park
B3. Red Crow Grille
B4. Chain motels
B5. The Lodge Hotel & Conference Center
B6. Whitey's

DAVENPORT
D1. Village of East Davenport
D2. Putnam Museum
D3. Credit Island Park
D4. Nahant Preserve and Recreation Area
D5. Interstate RV Park
D6. Casa Loma Inn & Suites
D7. motels at Brady Street near Interstate 80
D8. Hungry Hobo
D9. Harris Pizza
D10. Maid Rite
D11. Azteca
D12. Exotic Thai

ARSENAL ISLAND
A1. Old Fort Armstrong
A2. Mississippi River Visitor's Center
A3. Clock Tower
A4. first railroad bridge pier
A5. Colonel George Davenport House
A6. Rock Island Arsenal Museum
A7. Memorial Field
A8. Rock Island Confederate Cemetery/Rock
    Island National Cemetery

ROCK ISLAND
R1. Black Hawk State Historic Site/Hauberg
    Indian Museum
R2. Chippiannock Cemetery
R3. Boetje's Mustard
R4. Sunset Park
R5. Augustana College
R6. Looney's Roost
R7. Looney mansion/Frank Kelly house
R8. Jumer's Casino
R9. KOA Rock Island/Quad Cities
R10. Top O' the Morning
R11. 14th Avenue Waffle House
R12. La Rancherita
R13. Rock Island Public Library

MOLINE
M1. Sylvan Island
M2. John Deere World Headquarters
M3. motels near Quad City Airport
M4. RiverEdge Bed & Breakfast
M5. Maid Rite
M6. Exotic Thai

EAST MOLINE
E1. business district
E2. John Deere Harvester Works
E3. Campbell's Island State Historic Site
E4. Frieda's European Bakery and Tea Room
E5. Hungry Hobo

RIVER BOAT LANDINGS
L1. *Celebration Belle* pier
Channel Cat Water Taxi landings:
L1. Moline
L2. Isle of Capri landing, Bettendorf
L3. East Davenport
L4. John Deere Commons, Moline
L5. The Quarter

Quad Cities Overview
See separate city maps for more detail.

Davenport, Iowa

The dam at Lock and Dam 15

Sunset over the river.

Looney Mansion, Rock Island, Ill.

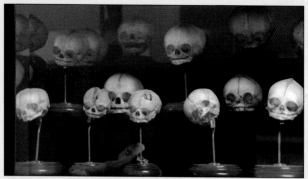

A display in the Palmer Osteological Collection, Palmer College

Rock Island Grand Prix

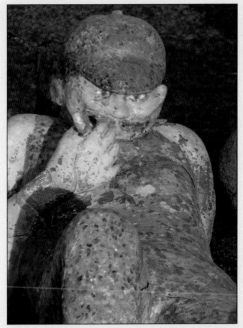

One of the Seurat-inspired characters at Credit Island Park

Davenport Skybridge

Joseph Bettendorf's mansion now houses Rivermont Collegiate private school, Bettendorf, Iowa.

John Deere headquarters, Moline, Illinois

PLEASANT VALLEY, IOWA

(Unincorporated)

Arriving in Town

US Highway 67 runs along the southern edge of the village. Valley Drive is the village's main drag; it parallels US 67.

Early History

European settlement in Pleasant Valley began when *Roswell Spencer* built a log cabin in 1833. The following winter, the family of *J.B. Chamberlin* moved into the very same cabin and stuck around long enough to be considered Pleasant Valley's first permanent settlers.

In 1840, the town tried to ensure its future relevance by bidding for the county seat, but, unfortunately for Pleasant Valley, they lost to Davenport. In 1856, Spencer, now a permanent resident, platted the village of Pleasant Valley, first calling it Valley City. In subsequent years he built a sawmill, a frame house, and a grist mill. Stones from the grist mill were used to build Trinity Lutheran Church, and the church later became the post office—the only one in the United States that is housed in a former church, for what it's worth. In spite of the village's early promise, growth was minimal and the town has never incorporated.

For much of its existence, Pleasant Valley was marked by a distinctive aroma—onions. In the 1850s, *Captain Isaac Hawley* planted the first crop. By 1858, several others had joined him and a robust onion farming industry had taken root. *Henry Schutter* arrived in 1856 and eventually became the most successful farmer of the bunch, managing hundreds of acres and earning the nickname "The Onion King."

The Pleasant Valley onion farmers were "organic" before organic was cool. They used homegrown seeds and developed their own varieties; weeds were picked by hand instead of being controlled with herbicides; farmers enriched their soil with manure instead of chemical fertilizers; onions were harvested manually instead of by machine. Onion farming lasted for generations, but a 1927 infestation of Yellow Dwarf virus led to a slow decline in the industry, as many farmers switched to other crops or moved out of the area. Even as the industry was waning, onion farming was an important safety net for many area families during the Depression. In the late 1990s, *Stanley Schutter*, the great grandson of "The Onion King," retired, closing the last remaining onion farm in the area.

Attractions

Lock and Dam 14 Recreation Area (182nd St.; 309.794.4524) is just two and a half miles south of I-80, which has a boat ramp, picnic tables, and two hiking trails. There is a rustic trail along the river that is accessed by the boat ramp, but a more interesting hike is the one-and-a-half mile trail on Smith Island. To reach the picnic tables and Smith Island, you get to walk across the top of a lock gate, in this case the auxiliary lock gate. Cool.

Resources

• Post Office: 24621 Valley Drive; 563.332.6232.

RIVERDALE, IOWA

(population 656)

Arriving in Town

US Highway 67 more or less bisects modest Riverdale.

Early History

Riverdale is barely two square miles of real estate that is surrounded by Bettendorf on three sides and by the Mississippi River on the other. A relative newcomer to the local incorporation scene, Riverdale came into being in the late 1940s after the Aluminum Company of America (Alcoa), completed its mile-long aluminum rolling mill along the riverfront, keeping alive a Quad Cities tradition of massive industrial sites next to the river. In 1948 the growing subdivisions attracted the attention of Bettendorf officials, who tried to annex the area. Residents objected, however, and in 1950 they filed a petition to incorporate as a separate town. The Iowa Supreme Court ended a three-year legal battle by ruling in favor of Riverdale.

BETTENDORF, IOWA

(population 31,275)

Arriving in Town

US Highway 67 enters Bettendorf on the southern part of town, then splits into two parallel one-way roads: Northbound US 67 (which technically goes in an easterly direction here) is Grant Street, while southbound US 67 (yes, it technically runs west) is State Street.

Early History

Early development moved slowly in the area that is now Bettendorf. In 1834, Dr. John Emerson staked a claim to land that is now at the foot of the twin bridges, but he died before he could develop it (see The Dred Scott Connection side story on page 53). A small section of what is now Bettendorf became known as Lillienthal, after the family that ran a tavern and dance hall. Lillienthal was later absorbed into the town of Gilbert, which was platted in 1858 by *Elias Gilbert*, the county surveyor. Gilbert, the town, was never incorporated, much to the disappointment of Gilbert, the surveyor, I bet. The area may have stayed a sleepy rural village if not for the arrival of two brothers and their industrial ambitions in 1902.

Brothers William and Joseph Bettendorf revolutionized an industry and changed the landscape of the Quad Cities in the process. William left home at age 13 and found a niche designing farm machinery. His first invention, the power-lift sulky plow, made life a lot easier for farmers; he added a simple gear mechanism which allowed the operator to lift the blade out of the

Map of Bettendorf

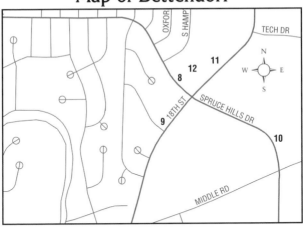

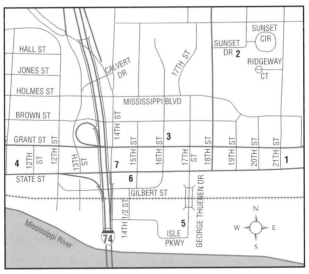

1. Old Bettendorf HQ
2. Rivermont Collegiate
3. Country Manor Chocolates
4. Waterfront Deli
5. Isle of Capri Casino
6. Twin Bridges Motor Inn/Paddle-
   wheel Sports Bar

7. Ross' 24-hour Family Restaurant
8. The Family Museum
9. Harris Pizza
10. Azteca 3
11. Bettendorf Post Office
12. Bettendorf Public Library

Note: The two maps connect via 18th St.

ground while seated. William also designed an all-
metal plow wheel; he was lured to Davenport in 1886
to construct a factory to build them. His younger
brother, Joseph, joined him in Davenport to help run
the business. For nearly 25 years, the Bettendorf brothers worked together in remarkable harmony—William
as the inventor genius and Joseph with the business
smarts.

The Bettendorfs suffered major setbacks in 1902
when fires destroyed their Davenport factory. Community leaders in Gilbert jumped on the opportunity.
They collected $15,000 to purchase a large tract of
land along the river and offered the land, free of cost,
to the Bettendorfs. They accepted. In April 1903,
grateful residents voted to incorporate under the name
Bettendorf.

Initially, the Bettendorf Company built steel wagon
gears and metal parts for farm machinery. Business
exploded after William designed a railroad car that
was cast in a single mold. Before William's invention,
railroad cars were constructed of several different parts
that were bolted together and therefore had limited
durability. William's invention was more stable and
proved very popular with the railroads. It also made
him and his brother very wealthy.

The number of Bettendorf employees grew from
300 in 1903 to 3,000 by 1920. Many of the early
workers were Armenian and Greek immigrants.
During World War I, however, the Bettendorfs faced
serious labor shortages. They responded by actively
recruiting hundreds of workers from Mexico. Most of
the Mexicans who arrived in Bettendorf lived in housing that was built by the company near the river. Their
neighborhood eventually became known as Holy City,
perhaps because many of the workers were renamed
"Jesus" by company employees who did not speak

Spanish well enough to understand their real names. The neighborhood was devastated by a flood in 1926, but descendents of many of those workers still live in the region.

Left, Joseph W. Bettendorf (courtesy of Davenport Public Library) and right, William P. Bettendorf (from *History of Davenport and Scott Co., Iowa*, by H.E. Downer)

The Bettendorf Company peaked between 1903 and 1933. Their success gave them the capital to purchase other businesses, like the Micro Company that successfully developed and marketed a bread-slicing machine that was sold to commercial bakeries around the world. Early machines for slicing bread had been developed by a few bakeries in Davenport, but the Micro Company gets credit for spreading the technology around the world. Yes, you could say sliced bread was invented in the Quad Cities.

Even with its manufacturing prowess and diversified interests, the Bettendorf Company was hit hard by the Depression—the factory closed in 1932 and Joseph died the following year. The complex was used to manufacture tanks in World War II, then sold to the J.I. Case Company before being demolishing in the 1950s for the construction of the second of the Twin

Bridges. *William Bettendorf*, son of Joseph, sold the last of the Bettendorf business interests in 1953, retiring the Bettendorf name from local industry. The town of Bettendorf has evolved from a gritty industrial town into a bedroom community, with a standard of living substantially higher than its neighbors.

Attractions

Two small parks are just north of Riverdale, hidden behind an industrial area. **Pigeon Creek Park** (6729 Shutters Lane; 563.344.4113) has a short hiking trail along the river and plenty of good spots to fish. It is closed to hikers between November and March to protect the habitat of bald eagles. Neighboring **Eagle's Landing Park** (2731 62nd Court; 563.344.4113) has a busy boat ramp and picnic tables and is a pleasant spot for river watching or fishing.

The only extant remnants of the **Bettendorf Company factory** are the foundry building just south of State Street at 23rd Street along the riverfront, now the Alter Bettendorf Warehouse (this is private property, so don't go wandering around without permission), and the art deco headquarters building at 2117 State Street.

Rivermont Collegiate (1821 Sunset Dr.; 563.359.1366; tours by appointment) is housed in the dignified mansion built for *Joseph Bettendorf*. The English Manor-inspired house was completed in 1915 on a 17-acre estate high on a bluff overlooking the river and the Bettendorf factory. The mansion was passed on to Joseph's son, William, who raised his family there. He sold the estate in 1959 to the Marist Society of D.C. which used it to house priests-in-training. In 1973, Rivermont Collegiate purchased the house. Rivermont was founded in 1884 as St. Katherine's, a boarding school for girls, and is now a non-sectarian private school educating girls and boys from preschool

Bettendorf, Iowa-Illinois Memorial Bridge

through high school; the mansion is part administrative office and part classroom.

The first floor still looks much as it was built and will give you a good sense of the Bettendorf tastes, including beautiful wood inlays, marble floors, an intricately carved staircase, and ceilings decorated with canvas paintings that were shipped to the mansion in finished form and installed. The south side of the house has a cement staircase guarded by well-sculpted marble dogs.

One curiosity about the mansion is that none of the fireplaces are functional. According to one story, Joseph suffered an eye injury during a blaze at his factory, which left him with a healthy fear of fire. When he built the mansion, he had fireplaces installed, but he insisted that they be decorative only. There is also a guest house on site that has a room decorated in an Egyptian theme. Rivermont Collegiate is happy to provide guided tours if you call in advance; summers are especially good times for tours as no classes are in session.

Country Manor Chocolates (412 16th St.; 866.810.2699/563.355.6600; M–F 10–6, Sa 10–4) is a family-run boutique chocolatier. Their hand made products include gorgeous truffles, sinful dark chocolates, and luscious chocolate-covered fruits. Stop in, sample, and stock up.

> ✔ **TIP: Bring your friends and take a 30-minute tasting tour ($3/person) or a kitchen tour where you may get to make your own chocolates ($5/person).**

The Family Museum (2900 Learning Campus Dr.; 563.344.4106; M–Sa 9–5, Su 12–5; $5) lives up to its name. Home to a collection of interactive exhibits about science and nature, such as Amazing Acres, where you can touch a ten-foot tornado or Busy Bodies where you can learn about the human body. Pre-teens will not be bored.

Entertainment ☼

Bettendorf is home for the **ISLE OF CAPRI CASINO** (1777 Isle Parkway; 800.724.5825/563.359.7280; Open 24 hours daily), 26,000 square feet of casino action (over 1,000 slot machines and 29 gaming tables) spread over several floors of a fake boat, plus a hotel, restaurants, and a marina.

Bars ♈

PADDLEWHEEL SPORTS BAR (at the Twin Bridges Motor Inn; 221 15th St.; 563.344.9646; open daily about 11-ish, closes around midnight on weekdays, 2 a.m. on weekends) hosts events such as the Outdoor Redneck Rodeo and is conveniently located next to the Twin Bridges Motor Inn, in case you have one beer too many.

Accommodations ⌂

• **THE TWIN BRIDGES MOTOR INN** (221 15th St.; 563.355.6451; $39 + tax) has tidy budget rooms near the Isle of Capri Casino. Patrons at the on-site bar occasionally get a bit loud. • Rooms at the **ISLE OF CAPRI** (1777 Isle Parkway; 800.843.4753; $69–$120 + tax) are pricier but put you in the middle of the casino action. • Another attractive option is **THE LODGE HOTEL & CONFERENCE CENTER** (I-74 & Spruce Hills Dr.; 866.690.4006/563.359.7141; $90–$195 + tax), with well-kept rooms and very attentive staff. • In addition to these places, there is a cluster of moderately priced major brands around I-74 & Kimberly Road.

Food ✗

ROSS' 24-HOUR FAMILY RESTAURANT (430 14th St.; 563.355.7573) is what family diners used to be like. The namesake Ross was the type of quick-witted character you hope to chat with over your morning coffee. One of his favorite gimmicks was serving bologna sandwiches on Election Day. How can you not respect that? If you are craving waffles in the morning (breakfast items $5–$7) or a fried banana split at 3 a.m., this is your place. If you are really hungry, try to scale the Magic Mountain ($6–$9), two feet of ground beef and fries atop Texas toast and drippin' with cheese sauce. Maybe it just seems like two-feet tall. Heck, they even have a bike rack. You'll need the extra exercise after eating here.

WATERFRONT DELI (1020 State St.; 563.359.4300; M–F 10–8, Sa 10–4) serves freshly-prepared salads ($3.50-$6.25) plus tasty sandwiches on bread baked in-house ($5-$6.25).

HARRIS PIZZA (2520 18th St.; 563.344.8727; Su–Th 11a–9p, F,Sa 11a–10p) created a style of pizza that is ubiquitous in the Quad Cities—cheesy, medium-thick crispy crust, slightly sweet and herby tomato sauce, and sometimes outlandish ingredients. Sure, you can get your basic pepperoni and mushroom, but why would you when you could have the Three Alarm Pizza (BBQ sauce, jalapeños, onions, and pepper jack cheese)? Don't forget the antacids. Harris Pizza has several locations around the Quad Cities.

AZTECA 3 (2400 Spruce Hills Dr.; 563.344.2121; M–Th 11–10, F 11–10:30, Sa 11:30–10, Su 11:30–9) is one of many fine, reasonably priced Mexican restaurants in the region, with good food and good service (most entrees <$8). They also have two locations in Davenport.

RED CROW GRILLE (2504 53rd Ave.; 563.332.2370; M–Th 5–10, F,Sa 5–11) offers a fine-dining experience that emphasizes high quality, seasonal ingredients (a la carte entrees $20–$31; most sides $4).

WHITEY'S ICE CREAM is a local institution that makes some of the best darn ice cream you will find, anywhere. They have several stores around town, most of which are not along the River Road. In Bettendorf, check out the store at 3515 Middle Road (563.332.4189; M-Th 10a-10p, F,Sa 10a-11p). A single scoop costs about $2 and a regular shake about $4.

Resources

- Post Office: 4439 Devils Glen Road; 563.332.6164.

- Bettendorf Public Library: 2950 Learning Campus Dr.; 563.344.4175; M–Th 9–9, F,Sa 9–5:30, Su 1–4 from Oct–Apr.

The Dred Scott Connection

Around 1834 Dr. John Emerson, the post surgeon for Fort Armstrong, made a claim on land in present-day Bettendorf. Dr. Emer- son brought along his slave, Dred Scott. While working at Fort Armstrong, Dr. Emerson became friends with Major Lawrence Taliaferro, who owned a slave named Harriet. The Major was trans-ferred to Fort Snelling, Minnesota, in 1835, as was Dr. Emerson when Fort Armstrong closed the next year. Late in 1836 Dred Scott married Harriet. Dred and Harriet were eventually sent back to St. Louis; they never returned to the Tri-Cities. Dr. Emerson left the Army in 1842, ready to develop his land claims on the north side of the Mississippi River, but his ambitions ended with his untimely death on December 29, 1843.

Dred Scott's time in Illinois, where slavery was illegal, was the basis for his later suit for freedom.

The Scotts filed their lawsuit against Dr. Emerson's widow, Irene, on April 6, 1846, based upon the doctrine of "once free, always free," a precedent that resulted in freedom for over 100 other slaves. A St. Louis jury awarded the Scotts their freedom in 1850, but the U.S. Supreme Court ruled in 1857 that the Scotts were personal property and should remain slaves, because the U.S. Constitution protected the property rights of U.S. citizens. The infamous decision inflamed the debate about slavery in the United States and made civil war nearly inevitable.

DAVENPORT, IOWA

(population 98,359)

Arriving in Town

After passing under I-74, you enter the City of Davenport, the largest municipality in the region. River Drive is the primary route next to the river, which is initially US Highway 67 but becomes US Highway 61 after the Centennial Bridge.

Early History

In the 1830s, two towns sprang to life on the Iowa bank of the Mississippi River. The village of Rockingham was settled in 1835 across from the mouth of the Rock River. The village seemed ideally located—except for the inconvenient fact that flooding turned the town into an island every year. In spite of its wet location, the village had 100 residents by the summer of 1836, twice as many as its neighbor, Davenport. The town of Davenport grew very slowly after its founding by *Antoine LeClaire*, using a contentious—and corrupt—victory over Rockingham for the county seat to solidify its future. In the first round of voting, Davenporters helped their cause by importing lead miners from Dubuque and paying them ten barrels of whiskey to vote. After two more controversial and equally corrupt elections, Davenport won the county seat and Antoine LeClaire donated land and $3,000 to build the first courthouse. Davenport annexed Rockingham a short time later.

Davenport became a port-of-call for steamboats very early, and by 1857, counted nearly 1,600 annual steamboat landings. Goods transported up the Missis-

Map of Downtown Davenport

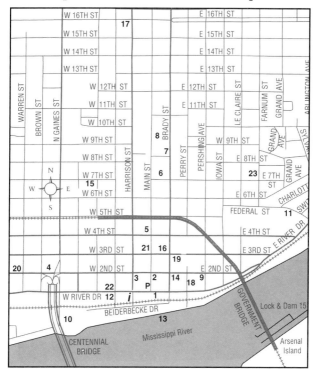

i - Union Station

P- Parking

1. Davenport Skybridge
2. River Music Experience/Mojo's/Redstone Room
3. Figge Art Museum
4. German American Heritage Center
5. St. Anthony Catholic Church
6. Palmer Museum of Chiropractic History
7. Palmer Mansion
8. David D. Palmer Health Sciences Library
9. Bucktown Center for the Arts
10. LeClaire Park/Modern Woodmen Park
11. Isabel Bloom Production Studio
12. Penguins Comedy Club/Nan's Piano Bar
13. Rhythm City Casino
14. Radisson Quad City Plaza
15. Beiderbecke Inn
16. Boozies Bar & Grill
17. Greatest Grains
18. Front Street Brewery
19. Duck City Bistro
20. Main Post Office
21. Davenport Public Library
22. Charles J. Wright Transit Center
23. Antoine LeClaire Historical Interpretive Center

sippi River supplied not only the immediate residents of the area but also farmers living in the fertile plains to the west. Davenport quickly grew into a regional commercial hub.

The arrival of thousands of Germans in the 1840s also gave Davenport a big boost. Most of the immigrants were political refugees from Schleswig-Holstein. They were wary of intimate church-state relations, largely because of the corruption they witnessed in that relationship in their homeland. When they arrived in America, they created private schools that were purely secular—a radical idea at the time. Many Germans were also deeply opposed to slavery and actively supported John Brown in his abolitionist pursuits.

The Germans brought with them a penchant for drinking and dancing on Sundays, something that the more staid Americans did not approve of. Egad! No wonder tensions were often high between the German immigrants and the second generation American families of Davenport.

Tensions dissipated after the Civil War, and a more unified community began to express its rebellious side. In 1884, the State of Iowa enacted an early version of Prohibition, but Davenport officials fought enforcement of the law within their boundaries. As Iowa continued to tinker with different enforcement mechanisms over the next 30 years, Davenport resisted at every step, ensuring that its residents lived in one of the few places in Iowa were alcohol could be purchased legally. Most of the taverns were confined to a four square-block district called Bucktown where the fun continued until sunrise at its 150 bars, 42 brothels, gambling halls, and boxing rings. Bucktown inspired Davenport's Bishop Henry Cosgrove to call his home town "the wickedest in the nation." Nothing like showing a little home town pride.

St. Anthony's Catholic Church in Davenport, Iowa.

After remarkable growth in the 19th century, Davenport's 35,000 residents had reason to feel good about their town. The 20th century, however, would be marked by continuing boom and bust periods. In the aftermath of World War I, Davenport residents looked for new leadership. In the 1920 municipal election, Davenport voters turned over city government to the Socialist Party, giving them the mayor's office and a majority on the city council. In-fighting ended their reign after only two years, however. The relationship between the mayor and the socialist aldermen became so poor that three aldermen bugged the mayor's office in an attempt to spy on him.

Attractions

Founded in 1851 to serve the logging industry, the **Village of East Davenport** (known locally as the East Village) was annexed by Davenport in 1856. The historic district has a collection of 19th century buildings that are now home to shops, restaurants, and bars.

The neighborhood also hosts several festivals during the summer. **Lindsay Park** (south side of 11th Street) is the site where Black Hawk camped before signing the Treaty of 1836 that ceded most of Iowa to the U.S. government and where artist George Catlin painted his portrait. The park has a good view of the river and is a nice spot for a picnic; free parking is available along 11th Street.

The Isabel Bloom Production Studio (736 Federal St.; 800.273.5436/563.336.3766; tours M @ 10a & 2nd & 4th Th @ 1p) makes sculptures out of cast concrete that are very popular with collectors. Even though I am not a fan of the pop-culture sentimentality of the figurines, I am awed by the production process—each figure is handcrafted and goes through a rigorous quality control process. Guided tours of the production facility take about an hour; advance reservations are required. They also have showrooms in East Davenport and Moline; see the shopping section for details.

In 1856, Antoine LeClaire built a solid brick home high atop a bluff overlooking the Mississippi Valley. That home is now the **Antoine LeClaire Historical Interpretive Center** (630 E. 7th St.). The house suffered through years of neglect but an ambitious rehab effort has restored much of the building. The main attraction inside is a collection of postcards showing Mississippi River towns around the turn of the 20th century. At this time, the interior is open for group tours only (call Karen at 563.324.0257 to arrange tours for large groups), but you are welcome to walk around the exterior of the home, picnic, and enjoy the views. Enter the parking lot via the alley on 8th Street.

Walking Tour of Downtown Davenport

Downtown attractions are close together and are therefore best explored on foot or by bike. Parking is plentiful in downtown Davenport. Spots at a street

The East Village neighborhood of Davenport, Iowa.

meter will cost you $1/hour with a two hour limit but street parking is free after 5 p.m. and on Saturday and Sunday. Your best bet during the day is probably the public garage across from the Figge Museum at River Drive and Main Street ($1/hour).

✔ **TIP: If you are up for a bike ride but don't have room to pack one, you can rent one between April and October at the Visitor's Center at Union Station (102 S. Harrison St.; 800.747.7800/563.322.3911; M–F 8:30–4:30, Sa,Su from June–Sept 10–4; $7/hour or $28/day). Bike rentals are also available at the Rock Island Centennial Bridge Visitors Center and the Moline Visitors Center.**

Once downtown, you may notice the **Davenport Skybridge** (Open 24 hours daily; free), that angular glass structure that stretches 600 feet and seems meant to deposit people at the casino's front door. Yes, that one. The views from the bridge are very good, especially on the south end. At night, the bridge is lit up in a variety of rotating colors. It's kinda cool, actually. Walk to the other end and return to the ground level via the stairs or elevator.

As you exit, walk through the courtyard, then to the

Daniel David Palmer, left, and son BJ, right
(Brett Marren)

The Palmers

Three generations of Palmers are largely respon-
sible for giving birth to and raising to adulthood
the chiropractic profession. Daniel David (D.D.)
Palmer was born near Toronto in 1845 but
migrated to the United States with his brother,
Thomas, after the American Civil War ended.
D.D. initially settled in New Boston, Ill., where
he raised bees.

In 1885, he moved to Davenport to open a
practice in "natural magnetic healing." Through
self-study and observation, he developed a theory
of disease that was way outside the mainstream
medical box. He came to believe that virtually
all disease was the result of the misalignment of
spinal vertebra or "sub-luxation" as he called it.
He believed that nerves transmitted not just basic
impulses but an intelligent, healing energy. Disease happened when sub-luxations blocked these
impulses from reaching internal organs.

His theory was put to the test in 1895 when he
popped the neck of Harvey Lillard, a janitor in
D.D.'s office building. Mr. Lillard had been deaf
for 17 years and traced his hearing loss back to
a day on which he heard a loud pop in his back
while stooped over. D.D. found a bump in

Lillard's vertebra and asked him to lie on a table face down. D.D. then gave a vigorous thrust into the back of Lillard's neck. Lillard reported that he could hear again immediately after the adjustment. D.D. and his friend, Reverend Samuel Weed, coined the term "chiropractic" for the new profession, a term derived from Greek that means "done by hand."

D.D. founded the Palmer School in 1897 and his son, B.J., joined him at the school shortly thereafter. However, the two had trouble collaborating and B.J. bought out his father in 1904. In the nearly 60 years that B.J. ran the Palmer School, he fought for the legitimization of chiropractic, built a professional school, and fought philosophical schisms in the emerging profession. Nevertheless, he guided the Palmer School's development into a full-fledged professional school with active clinical and research programs. B.J.'s wife, Mabel, also was active in the Palmer School as the resident anatomy expert and a popular teacher.

B.J. was a true eccentric. He slept irregularly, often waking in the middle of the night with an idea that he would immediately start working on. He had lived around the circus as a child and remained fond of it throughout his life, even building a room in his house that resembled a big tent and retiring near Sarasota, Florida, near the winter home of the Barnum & Bailey circus.

The third Palmer, David D., took the reins at the Palmer School after B.J.'s death in 1961 and renamed it the Palmer College of Chiropractic. He modernized the campus, established the college as a non-profit entity, and founded an alumni association. Shortly after his death in 1978, the Palmer College received full accreditation.

left and go to the **River Music Experience** (129 W. 2nd St.; 877.326.1333/563.326.1333; Open M–Th 7a–9p, F 7a–10p, Sa 10a–10p; free). Go in. Now. The first floor houses Mojo's Coffeehouse (563.326.1555; same hours as the RME), where you can get yourself a latte, scone, and a B.B. King CD. The museum is on the second floor.

The River Music Experience (aka the RME) is best experienced by listening, appropriately enough, at one of eight stations. Each station highlights a Mississippi River port-of-call, describing the styles of music emanating from that area and the musicians who made it famous. Don't rush here. Take your time; listen and enjoy. While the museum has a heavy dose of jazz and blues, as one would expect, other styles of music receive ample attention, as well. If you are an aspiring musician and happen to be between eight and 18 years old, the RME hosts Rock Camp several times during the summer, two weeks of intense training to kick start your rock star career. The RME is also home to the best live music venue in the Quad Cities—the Redstone Room (see the Entertainment section later in this chapter).

✔ **TIP: If only bright, shiny, quickly moving things keep your attention, the RME is not the best place for you. You won't enjoy your visit unless you camp out at the listening stations and get comfortable.**

Exit the River Music Experience and continue west (left) on 2nd Street, a stretch of several blocks that is part sculpture garden. Your next stop is the **Figge Art Museum** (225 W. 2nd St.; 563.326.7804; Tu,W,F–Su 10–5, Th 10–9; $7), the large glass structure that looks something like a fragile towboat. One hour should be enough time to see the highlights, which include a colorful collection of Haitian art, an intriguing juxtaposition of Mexican and Haitian altars, two paintings by native Midwesterner Thomas Hart Benton, and, for a touch of local river history, the painting "Old Ferry—View of Rock Island Blockhouse 1846" by John Caspar Wild. The latter paintings are housed in the collections of 19th/20th century European/American art.

✔ TIP: If you would like to explore more of the museum, consider arranging a guided theme tour ($7/person), like Artist Materials that focuses on mediums and techniques or Art of Lettering that focuses on calligraphy and gives you a chance to learn a few strokes, too. Specialty tours should be arranged two weeks in advance.

Walk five blocks farther west to the **German American Heritage Center** (712 W. 2nd St.; 563.322.8844; Tu–Su 1–4; $3). Many of the early immigrants to this area were Germans who were escaping political upheaval and economic collapse at home. At the German American Heritage Center, you can read about the various waves of German immigration and their influence on the Quad Cities (and much of the United States).

Walk back to Main Street and turn left (north) on Main. Two blocks up and on the right is **St. Anthony Catholic Church** (417 Main St.; 563.322.3303; by appointment; free), the first Catholic parish in Davenport. The original church was built in 1838 by *Father Samuel Mazzuchelli*, with support from Antoine LeClaire; that building is currently the parish religious education center. Because of an onslaught of migration to Davenport, a bigger church was needed. The new building was completed in 1853 and is still in use. The sanctuary is only open to the public about 30 minutes before a mass (Sa 5p; Su 7a, 8:30a, 10a, 11:30a); otherwise, call ahead to schedule a tour of the interior.

Continue walking north on Main Street to the campus of the **Palmer College of Chiropractic**. I love this place! The founders were fascinating, quirky people (see the side story on pages 60-61), and the college today wears its eccentricities with pride. Begin your circuit through chiropractic history by turning right on 7th Street and walking two blocks to Vickie Ann Palmer Hall (formerly Lyceum Hall).

Inside the building is the **Palmer Museum of Chiropractic History** (Palmer Hall, 115 W. 7th St.; 563.884.5245; M–F 8–4:30, by appt at other times; free). In 1895, *Daniel David Palmer* popped the back of one Harvey Lillard at his office in downtown Davenport, thus performing the first known chiropractic adjustment. In 1906 D.D. Palmer was jailed for 23 days for practicing medicine without a license, an event that recurred across the country and launched a movement to legitimize the profession of chiropractic. Museum displays are scattered about Palmer Hall, but you will find most of them in the basement and first floor lobby. In the basement, there is a display case with a variety of animal skeletons, another case describing the historical context when chiropractic emerged, and a giant clam shell. In the first floor lobby, there is a replica of the office used by D.D. Palmer plus an exhibit commemorating the centennial of the profession of chiropractic that includes adjustment tables from every decade.

One block north is the **Palmer Mansion** (8th & Main Streets; 563.884.5404; F 11 a.m. or by appt.; free), a fine example of what happens when eccentricity is blessed with wealth. During the first part of the tour, I was lulled into thinking this was just another ordinary rich person's home, but once I entered the enclosed porch, I quickly changed my mind. The porch has a number of curiosities, including a built-in pipe organ that still works, stunning examples of forbidden stitch embroidery, a room made to resemble the big tent at a circus, and a chair whose legs are made from genuine elephant feet. The courtyard has a few remnants of the once hugely popular stone garden called A Little Bit O' Heaven. Part greenhouse and part spiritual funhouse, the garden drew a steady stream of visitors until the death of B.J. Palmer, when it fell into disrepair. It was eventually razed. Remaining pieces include La Petite Chapelle, aka the "World's Smallest Church," the Wishing Buddha, and Hindu statues from Bali.

If that's not enough eccentricity for you, B.J. Palmer had a thing for collecting bones; he used them as teaching aids. Starting with a handful of skeletons he acquired from his father, he accumulated thousands of samples, many of which are disturbingly contorted and deformed. These bones form the **Palmer Osteological Collection**; pieces are available for viewing in scattered locations around the campus. Apart from the displays in the Palmer Museum in the Palmer Hall basement, the most accessible display cases are in the basement of the David D. Palmer Health Sciences Library (Main Street near Palmer Drive; 563.884.5896 for reference desk; regular hours are M–Th 7:15a–11p, F 7:15a–5p, Sa 9–5, Su 3p–11p but hours vary with the academic calendar—call to confirm). The display cases are full of feet, hands, skulls, and spines contorted into shapes that just aren't right. Other display cases are located in the Campus Health Center in B.J. Palmer Hall but please get permission at the front desk to visit the displays.

If you wander around the campus, you might notice a number of epigrams painted on the walls. B.J. Palmer had a thing for creating and collecting these catchy turns-of-phrase. Some fun ones include:

"A 'specialist' is one who knows more and more about less and less."

"A wise man never blows his knows."

"An optimist is the one who sees a light where there is none. A pessimist is one who blows it out."

✔ **TIP:** You can see a large collection of B.J. Palmer's epigrams painted on the wall of the breezeway between the Palmer Mansion and the West Hall Courtyard.

Walk back toward the river (south) on Brady Street to 2nd Street, turn left (east) and finish your walking tour at the **Bucktown Center for the Arts** (225 E. 2nd St.; 563.324.1005; W–Sa 11–6; free), a 19th-century commercial building now turned into an arts incubator. The center is located in the once-infamous entertainment district that was essentially closed by the federal government in 1918 when, in an attempt to protect its war-time workforce—from vice, presumably—it ordered the closure of all saloons and "bawdy houses" within a half-mile of the Rock Island Arsenal.

The Arts Center houses a collection of shops filled with works created by local visual artists. The quality is generally high and the prices reasonable. **MidCoast Fine Arts** (309.737.2066) maintains a small, second-floor gallery exhibiting works by local artists.

If you are in no hurry and the weather is nice, this would be a great place to relax and enjoy the riverfront. **LeClaire Park** has a bandshell and is the site of many summer festivals. Next door is **Modern Woodmen Park**, a baseball stadium completed in 1931 and home to the minor league Quad Cities River Bandits. On the other side of the bridge is a skate park. The paved walking/bicycling path extends westward to Credit Island Park and eastward to the Isle of Capri Casino in Bettendorf.

Other Davenport Sights

If you only have time to visit one museum in the Quad Cities, go the River Music Experience. If, however, you have time for a second one, tour the **Putnam Museum** (1717 W. 12th St.; 800.435.3701/563.324.1933; M–Th 11–5; F,Sa 11–7, Su 12–5; $6) for its excellent exhibits on natural and cultural history. River, Prairie, and People covers the region's history, from pre-colonial times to the present. Black Earth/Big River is an interactive exhibit about the ecology of the Mississippi River valley. The museum also has an IMAX theater with rotating shows.

Credit Island Park (2500 W. River Dr; 563.326.7812), the site of an early French trading post, is a good spot to rest your feet and good for people watching, too. It is also home to one of the area's more unusual attractions: the nearly life-size wooden sculptures created by artist Thom Gleich that were inspired by the characters from Seurat's painting, "A Sunday Afternoon on the Island of La Grande Jatte."

Nahant Preserve, Education, and Recreation Area (4220 S. Wapello Ave.; 563.326.7766; grounds open daily sunrise to sunset; Education Center generally open M–F 8–5; free) is a 513-acre preserve created on the site of a former shooting range. A cooperative effort between public and private agencies helped to remove hazardous amounts of lead and restore the marsh. The preserve has a couple of short walking trails and viewing platforms good for bird-watching, especially during migration season.

Entertainment ⚐

THE PENGUINS COMEDY CLUB (421 W. River Dr..; 563.324.5233; Th 7:30p, F 8p, Sa 7:30p,10p) hosts stand-up comics, many nationally known, for weekend shows in the historic Freight House building on the Davenport riverfront.

Davenport's **RHYTHM CITY CASINO** (101 W. River Dr.; 800.262.8711/563.322.2628; Open 24 hours daily) floats on a boat along the downtown riverfront. It has 35,000 square feet of gaming, with about 1,000 slot machines and 28 gaming tables.

Live Music ⌨

At the **REDSTONE ROOM** (129 Main St.; 563.326.1333), located on the second floor of the **RIVER MUSIC EXPERIENCE**, the patrons are not smoking but the performers are. Drawing regional and national musicians, this is the best venue in the Quad Cities for live music. Some shows sell out, so you may want to buy tickets in advance. MOJO'S (563.326.1555; M–Th 7a–9p, F 7a–10p, Sa 10–10), on the first floor of the RME, also hosts live music throughout the week.

NAN'S PIANO BAR (421 W. River Dr., Freight House 2nd floor; 563.323.5081; Su,Tu–Th 4:30–midnight; F,Sa 4:30–2a; F,Sa cover charge of $5–$7), in the same building as the Penguins Comedy Club, is just what it sounds like—a bar with a focus on pianists; some weekend performances feature pianists dueling for the crowd's affection.

Bars ♀

Rumor has it that the **11TH STREET PRECINCT BAR & GRILL** (2108 E. 11th St.; 563.324.9545; bar open daily 11a–2a) in East Davenport can be a fun place to hang out, with live music on weekend nights that attracts a largely baby boomer crowd. (See also under "Food.")

THE FRONT STREET BREWERY (208 E. River Dr.; 563.322.1569; Su–Th 11:30–11, F,Sa 11:30–midnight), located in the heart of the old Bucktown district, produces fine craft beers like the Raging River Ale in a laid-back atmosphere. (See also under "Food.")

Don't be fooled by the posters of musicals on the walls at **BOOZIES** (114½ West 3rd St.; 563.328.2929; M–F open until midnight-ish, Sa open until 2a, Su 12–8). You won't hear "Ol' Man River" here. The after-work crowd of devout regulars turns over later in the evening for a crowd that is mostly students from the Palmer Chiropractic College and St. Ambrose University. (See also under "Food.")

DAM VIEW INN (410 East 2nd St.; 563.322.1605; M–F 2p–2a Sa,Su 11a–2a) has a pool table, cheap beer, and friendly people. On Tuesday nights you can get pitchers for $3 as well as some kind of apple-flavored shot that I know I tasted but don't really remember. The Dam View Inn usually draws a mixed crowd of college students and working stiffs.

Davenport has two gay bars: **MARY'S ON 2ND** (832 W. 2nd St.; 563.884.8014; daily 2p–2a) feels like a neighborhood bar but with more attitude, while **CLUB FUSION** (813 W. 2nd St.; 563.326.3452; daily 4p–2a) is the place to dance.

Shopping 💳

The East Village has several specialty shops that are worth a diversion, including: • **AVATAR BOOKS** (2218 E. 11th St.; 563.322.4159; M–Sa 11–5), a fine source for used and collectible books; • **CAMP MCCLELLAN CELLARS** (2302 E. 11th St.; 563.322.2100; M,Tu,Sa 10–5, W–F 10–6), selling locally produced wines and supplies for home-brewing and home winemaking; • **ESTATE WINES** (2218 E. 11th St.; 563.326.6059; M,W 12–6, Tu,Th 11:30–6, F,Sa 11:30–7), which specializes in premium wines from New York; • **ISABEL BLOOM** (1109 Mound

St.; 563.324.5135; M–F 10–6, Sa 10–5, Su 12–4),
selling handcrafted cast concrete sculptures; visit
• **THE SOAP BOX** (2033 E. 11th St.; 563.322.4096;
M–Sa 10–5) for self-pampering goodies like fine soaps
and body-care products; • **YOUR HEART'S DESIRE**
(2119 E. 12th St.; 563.322.0546; M–Sa 10–5) sells
handcrafted soaps and candles, gourmet food items,
and old-fashioned candies for the kids; • **BLUE SKY**
(1018 Mound St.; 563.650.8887; M–F 10–5, Sa
10–4, Su 12–3) has an eclectic collection of home
furnishings and stuff meant to make you laugh.

In Downtown Davenport, • **RIVER BEND AN-
TIQUES** (419 Brady St.; 563.323.8622; M–Sa 10–5,
Su 12–4) is a warren of rooms and closets loaded with
antiques, memorabilia, and lots of other stuff you
never knew you needed. • **THE SOURCE BOOK
STORE** (232 W. 3rd St.; 563.324.8941; M–F 9:30–
5:30, Sa 9:30–5) is the authority on used books in the
area. They have a good sampling of books on local
history and on the Mississippi River, plus many others
in the thousands of titles available.

• **NORTHPARK MALL** is in northern Davenport
(320 W. Kimberly Rd; 563.391.4500; M-Sa 10-9, Su
Noon-6); it's a bit creepy in a neglected and lifeless
way, but, hey, it's a mall.

Accommodations ⌂

Davenport has two campgrounds: • **INTERSTATE
RV PARK** (8448 Fairmount St.; 888.387.6573/
563.386.7292), just north of I-80 at Northwest
Blvd., has 98 sites for RVs ($27–$33). • **LAKESIDE
RV PARK & CAMPGROUND** (11279 140th St.;

563.381.3413) is opposite town at I-280 and Iowa Highway 22; it has 22 sites ($15–$17).

Lodging options in downtown Davenport are limited to the upscale • **RADISSON QUAD CITY PLAZA** (111 E. 2nd St.; 888.201.1718/563.322.2200; $129–$169; WiFi). Other fine options in Davenport include the • **BEIDERBECKE INN** (532 W. 7th St.; 866.300.8858/563.323.0047; $85–$105 + tax incl full breakfast & WiFi), a handsome bed-and-breakfast in the house built by the grandparents of Bix Beiderbecke, and the • **CASA LOMA INN & SUITES** (6014 N. Brady St.; 888.386.1293/563.386.1290; $65–$94 + tax; WiFi), with its log and stone décor. • The Casa Loma's neighborhood—Brady Street near Interstate 80— has a number of budget to mid-range chain motels that are a ten-minute drive from downtown Davenport.

Food ✖

Get your java fix at **MOJO'S** at the River Music Experience (129 W. 2nd St.; 563.326.1555; M–Th 7a–9p, F 7a–10p, Sa 10–10), which also serves sandwiches (<$7) and has free WiFi.

In the East Village, the **BIER STUBE** (2228 E. 11th St.; 563.323.2174; M–Th 11–10, F,Sa 11–11, Su 11–9), a smaller version of the popular Moline restaurant, serves German-inspired dishes (entrees $7–$13.50). (See the Moline entry for more info.)

11TH STREET PRECINCT BAR AND GRILL (2108 E. 11th St.; 563.324.9545; M–Sa 11–9:30, Su 11–9) serves sandwiches ($4.50–$8.50) and pizza. Check out the pork tenderloin sandwich, which violates all kinds of Midwestern cooking rules by not being breaded and fried.

LAGOMARCINOS (2132 E. 11th St.; 563.324.6137; M–Sa 9–5:30) has a more celebrated location in Moline, but this one serves up the same delicious homemade ice cream, hot fudge sundaes, and old-school sodas.

Locals flock to **HUNGRY HOBO**, a hometown sandwich shop ($3-$5.50) with several stores around the area. Bread and soup are made fresh daily. In Davenport, the store closest to the river road is on East Locust at Bridge Avenue (1145 E. Locust St.; 563.322.2347; M–F 11-8, Sa,Su 11-7).

BOOZIES BAR & GRILL (114 ½ W. 3rd St.; 563.328.2929; M–Sa 11a–10p) consistently gets props for its burgers ($6.50–$8), especially the namesake Boozie Burger topped with bacon, a trio of cheeses, and just about anything else you could want. If you are not in the mood for a burger, they have an assortment of other pub-inspired sandwiches and entrees ($6–$12).

HARRIS PIZZA (see the description in the Bettendorf section) has two locations in Davenport, one on the west side (1601 W. 3rd St.; 563.326.3551) and another on the east side (524 E. Locust St.; 563.322.2411); both are open the same hours (Su–Th 11–9:30, F,Sa 11–10:30).

GREATEST GRAINS (1600 N. Harrison; 563.323.7521; M–Sa 9–8, Su 10–7) is a small grocery store that specializes in health-food products, including a wide selection of organic foods. They also have a decent selection of inexpensive prepared foods like sandwiches, wraps, soups, and salads ($2–$6).

FRONT STREET BREWERY (208 E. River Dr.; 563.322.1569; Su–Th 11:30–11, F,Sa 11:30–midnight) serves up a range of salads, sandwiches ($4.50–$9), and above average pub-grub entrees ($8–$15). My personal favorite is the Porterhouse Pork Chop ($13).

MAID RITE (1622 Rockingham Rd.; 563.322.2881; M–F 6a–7p, Sa 6a–5p, Su 7a–2p) is a regional favorite that specializes in seasoned ground beef on a bun, kinda like a sloppy joe, except without the sauce (about $3). Get one with everything, including ketchup.

AZTECA has two Davenport locations: one in Walnut Center (4811 N. Brady St.; 563.386.6689) and another on the east side (2801 E 53rd St.; 563.386.6689), both open the same hours (M–Th 11–10, F 11–10:30, Sa 11:30–10, Su 11:30–9) and both serving quality, affordable Mexican food (most entrees <$8).

EXOTIC THAI (2303 E. 53rd St.; 563.344.0909; M–F 11–3,5–10, Sa,Su 11–10) is a bit out of the way but well worth the trip. They serve very good Thai dishes (entrees $8–$15) in an attractive setting. They have another location in Moline.

The attentive staff at **DUCK CITY BISTRO** (115 E. 3rd St.; 563.322.3825; M-Sa 5p-10p) serves inspired food in a laid-back atmosphere. Core entrees include paella and steaks ($16–$25), but the real thrill is in the specials ($30+). On a cold November night I enjoyed three shrimp, each the size of my fist—can that still be called "shrimp"? —surrounded by a curry sauce and resting on half of a roasted butternut squash ($39). If you want a special meal, consider coming here.

Resources

- Main Post Office: 933 W. 2nd St.; 563.323.0306.
- Davenport Public Library—Main Branch: 321 Main St.; 563.326.7832; M,Th 12–8, Tu,W,F,Sa 9:30–5:30.

ARSENAL ISLAND, ILLINOIS

Arriving on Arsenal Island

Arsenal Island is connected to Davenport by the Government Bridge and Rock Island and Moline via causeways. There are several attractions on the island and most are accessible from the main road (Rodman Avenue).

This is a military installation but the public is welcome to visit the island; you just need to show a photo ID and tell them your destination (be specific: for example, the Mississippi River Visitor's Center or the Arsenal Museum), and they will give you a pass to enter. If you are not a U.S. Citizen, you will need to present your passport at the gate. During business hours, you will be directed to the visitor's center for a background check; at other times, the guard will perform the check. The process usually takes from 30 minutes to two hours.

✔ TIP: A quick note for bicyclists: you can NOT ride a bicycle onto Arsenal Island unless you are an employee. However, you can throw your bike on your car, drive onto the island, then remove your bike and ride around. Don't ask me—I don't understand it, either. Frankly, though, they don't really want you riding your bike around the Island, especially on the main roads. If you choose to do so, anyway, wear a helmet—federal law requires it—and stick to the secondary roads on the northern end of the Island.

Early History

The United States acquired title to Arsenal Island in 1804 through a treaty with the Sauk and Mesquakie, although the validity of the treaty was challenged by those Indian nations for many years (see page 13). The first military outpost, Fort Armstrong, was built on the western end of the island in 1816. *George Davenport* ran the fort's commissary and lived a short distance away. The fort served as military headquarters during the Black Hawk War, but closed just four years after the war ended. The Army used the fort's buildings as a weapons depot until 1845. The last remnants of the

fort were razed in 1864.

The U.S. government lost interest in the island until the Civil War. After Confederate troops

Ordnance Depot 1943 (by permission of the U.S. Army, Rock Island Arsenal Museum, Rock Island, Illinois)

destroyed the Harper's Ferry Armory in 1861, the Union needed a safe location to store armaments. A lobbying effort by local officials coupled with astute political maneuvering persuaded Congress to create the Rock Island Arsenal in 1862. The new arsenal was quickly called to serve an unintended purpose: prison camp for captured Confederate soldiers. At its peak, nearly 8,600 Confederate soldiers were housed on the island. Rotating groups of soldiers served as prison guards, including a turn by the 108th Regiment, U.S. Colored Infantry. I'm sure that went over well with the Confederate troops. Between 1863 and 1865, about 2,000 Confederate POWs died at the Rock Island camp, mostly from diseases such as smallpox and pneumonia.

Major Charles Kingsbury, the Arsenal's first commander, began construction of the first building, now known as the Clock Tower, in 1863, but a number of logistic and financial challenges delayed completion until 1867. The Arsenal's second commander, *Brevet Brigadier General Thomas Rodman*, laid out the grand

plans that gave the installation its current shape: a group of ten large workshops, quarters for the commanding officer, and a bridge that would connect the island to Iowa. Rodman died unexpectedly in 1871, but his plans were completed by his successor, *Lieutenant Colonel Daniel Flagler*.

Brigadier General Thomas Rodman (by permission of the U.S. Army, Rock Island Arsenal Museum, Rock Island, Illinois)

The ten shops, each covering a full acre, were built with imposing limestone facades; they are still in use today. Quarters One, home for the commanding officer, was completed just after Rodman died. The ornate Italianate building has 19,000 square feet of living space, making it the second-largest single-family home in the government's real-estate portfolio; only the White House is larger. The bridge Rodman envisioned was completed in 1872, then completely overhauled in 1896.

For the first dozen years of its existence, the Arsenal was only authorized to serve as a depot. In 1875, however, it manufactured its first items for the Army and continues to do so to this day. For the most part, the Arsenal has produced small arms like howitzers, rifles, rocket launchers, and machine guns, in addition to supplies like mess kits, harnesses, and canteen carriers. The main products manufactured at the Arsenal now are gun mounts, recoil mechanisms, artillery cartridges, and tools for field repairs. The Arsenal has been a major employer for the region since its inception but especially during war time. During WWII, employment peaked at nearly 19,000 but has more typically been around 2,000 in peacetime.

Attractions

Just outside the guard shack, there is a replica, built in 1916, of a blockhouse from the Old Fort Armstrong and a sculpture called **The Gathering Point**. There are a handful of parking spots near the blockhouse.

Immediately on your left after passing through the guard shack is the **Mississippi River Visitor's Center** (Building 328, Rodman Ave.; 800.645.0248/309.79 4.5338; daily 9–5, Sa,Su 9–7 from Memorial Day to Labor Day; free), host to several displays that highlight Mississippi River ecology and commerce. This is also a good vantage point to watch barges pass through Lock 15, which was the first of 29 built that aimed to tame the Mississippi River for navigation.

In the Quad Cities, the completion of **Lock and Dam 15** buried the hazardous rapids and created a large lake that is popular with recreational boaters. The pool behind this dam is one of the most stable in the system; the water level only fluctuates by one to three feet, even during floods, an ironic turn of fate—from being one of the most hazardous stretches of the river to navigate to being one of the most dependable.

✓ **TIP: During summer weekends, roughly from Memorial Day to Labor Day, the Army Corps of Engineers offers free guided tours of the lock (Sa,Su 11a,2p), but you must call ahead to reserve a spot. They also offer guided bicycle tours around the island; check the schedule for dates or give them a call.**

As you exit the visitor's center, look across the street and up at the six-story **Clock Tower**. The tower was built of native limestone and was part of the first structure built for the Arsenal. The clock was purchased from New York-based A.S. Hotchkiss Company and installed in 1868. Each of the four clock faces is 12 feet in diameter; the minute hands are six feet long and the second hands are five feet long. The clock still has its original parts and still works. If the clock doesn't interest you, the views from the top floor are the best in the Quad Cities. The Corps leads tours through the Clock Tower, but reservations are required (800.645 .0248/309.794.5338); you can also arrange tours for other times but only if you have a group of at least ten people and book two or more weeks in advance.

Just east of the lock and dam, there is a stone monument marking the location of one of the piers of the first railroad bridge across the Mississippi River (see side story on page 91).

The Colonel George Davenport House (Hillman St.; 309.786.7336; Th–Su 12–4; $5) was constructed in 1833 and was the center of civic life in the region for years: Rock Islanders plotted to get the county seat here, towns were platted, and leaders negotiated with railroad executives for a rail port. On July 4, 1845, Colonel Davenport was at home when several men entered the house. During the robbery, Davenport was shot and mortally wounded. The murder shocked and angered the community, which launched a massive

manhunt. Six men were eventually caught and convicted. On October 29, just three months after the murder, three of the men were hanged in a public square
before a large crowd. In a bizarre twist, the rope broke
for one of the men and the executioner had to reload
and try again, while fending off cries from the gallery
that the broken rope was a sign from God to halt the
execution. Even though several men were caught and
executed for the crime, rumors persist to this day that
Davenport's murder was part of a larger conspiracy to
kill him, although the motivation for such a conspiracy
often varies from story to story.

The Rock Island Arsenal Museum (North Ave.;
309.782.5021; Tu–Su 10–4; free) is the second-oldest
U.S. Army Museum; it has been open since 1905. The
collection includes an impressive number and diversity
of handguns, rifles, and other small arms.

Memorial Field (Rodman Ave. at East Ave.;
309.782.5021; daily sunrise–sunset; free) is an outdoor
museum of sorts, with a collection of ordnance systems, including artillery pieces and rocket launchers.
Most of the weapons on display were manufactured on
the island at one time.

Farther down Rodman Avenue you will find **Rock
Island Confederate Cemetery** and then **Rock Island
National Cemetery**. The Confederate Cemetery is
the final resting place for nearly 2,000 Confederate
soldiers who died while imprisoned on the island
during the Civil War. The national cemetery began in
1863 as the burial grounds for Union soldiers guard-
ing that same Confederate prison camp. Over 29,000
veterans and their relatives are interred here. Both
cemeteries are free and open daily from sunrise to
sunset (309.782.2094).

ROCK ISLAND, ILLINOIS

(population 39,684)

Arriving in Town

The River Road snakes through Rock Island first as the Rock Island Expressway, then as 1st, 5th, and 7th Avenues.

Early History

In 1833, the Illinois legislature created Rock Island County with the county seat to be located at a city called Stephenson. (The name was chosen to honor *Colonel Benjamin Stephenson*, a veteran of the Black Hawk War. An earlier attempt to name the town after Colonel Davenport, who was the new town's most prominent citizen, failed when a legislator objected because the Colonel had criticized U.S. conduct during the Black Hawk War.) Stephenson was platted in 1835 and had 600 residents by 1840. In 1841, the name was changed to Rock Island, and the new town expanded by annexing territory that included the neighboring town of Farnhamsburg.

Following consolidation in 1841, Rock Island grew into a transportation and manufacturing center. The first railroad reached town in 1854, just as steamboat traffic peaked at 175 landings every month. *Charles Buford* founded the Buford Plow Company in the mid-1800s, kicking off farm implement manufacturing in the region, arguably the most important industry in the Quad Cities. By the 1870s, Rock Island was the center of three big railroads that connected the city

Map of Downtown Rock Island

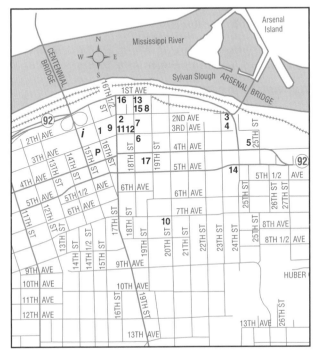

i - Centennial Bridge Visitor Center

P - Parking

1. MidCoast Fine Arts Left Bank Gallery
2. Quad Cities Arts
3. Liquid Fire Studio
4. Quad Cities Wood Turners
5. Quad City Botanical Center
6. Comedy Sportz
7. Huckleberry's Pizza & Calzones
8. RIBCO
9. Holiday Inn Rock Island/ Quad Cities
10. Victorian Inn
11. Theo's Java Club
12. Mama Compton's
13. Blue Cat Brew Pub
14. Jim's Rib Haven
15. Atlante Trattoria
16. Le Figaro French Restaurant
17. Rock Island Public Library

to markets from New York to San Francisco, while the Mississippi River ensured access to markets from Minneapolis to New Orleans. The growth of the railroad business in Rock Island was helped by the construction of a railroad bridge in 1856.

In the early 20th century, Rock Island was more or less ruled by a mobster named *John Looney* (see side

Chippiannock Cemetery, Rock Island

story on pages 84-85), who cultivated a culture of fear and corruption that dominated the city. The city's reputation was so foul that when future-President *Woodrow Wilson* visited the region in April 1912, he moved the location of his speech from raucous Rock Island to mild-mannered Moline.

Attractions

Voted one of the Seven Wonders of Illinois, the **Black Hawk State Historic Site** (1510 46th Ave.; 309.788.0177; daily sunrise–sunset) is one part historic site and two parts park. For the history part, the modest **Hauberg Indian Museum** (309.788.9536; W–Su 9–noon, 1–5; $2 suggested donation), located inside the impressive lodge built by the Civilian Conservation Corps in the 1930s, has dioramas displaying Sauk and Mesquakie life in the 18th century. To explore the park, just walk around. A wide range of wildflowers add a dramatic touch to the landscape between mid-April and mid-May. Black Hawk Prairie is west of the lodge, a small area set aside to replicate the type of tallgrass prairie that once dominated the landscape here.

When it comes to the architecture devoted to memorializing the dead, few places have impressed me more than **Chippiannock Cemetery** (12th St. at 29th Ave.; 309.788.6622; daily 8a–sunset; free). You are welcome to stop at the office and pick up a map, but wandering aimlessly can be very rewarding. Most of the older sections will be on your left as you enter the cemetery and then to the right and up the hill. The markers are a testament to the incredible carving skills of stone masons: a cloth draped delicately on a marker, a perfectly chiseled anvil, a chalice supported by tree limbs. *Colonel Davenport* and his family are buried here; their graves are marked by a simple obelisk near the top of the hill. Also interred here is lumber baron *Frederick Weyerhaeuser*. Perhaps the most remarkable memorial, though, is dedicated to siblings *Eddie and Josie Dimich*, who were five and nine years old, respectively, when they died from diphtheria on the same evening in 1878. The children had a devoted pet dog, a Newfoundland, who used to follow the children everywhere. After the children died the dog would make the short walk from home to the cemetery every day until he himself died, or so the story goes. Regardless, when the dog died, the children's father commissioned a stone carver to create an image of the dog and had it placed next to his children's graves.

As long as you're in the neighborhood, pay a visit to a local institution—**Boetje's Mustard** (2736 12th St.; 309.788.4352; Tours June–September by appointment), just across the street from the cemetery. Boetje's

John Looney

Every town needs a good villain in its history. Rock Island has John Looney. He moved to Rock Island in the mid-1880s to work for the Rock Island & Peoria Railroad and entered the law profession two years later. In 1900 he founded a newspaper called the *Rock Island News*, which put the yellow in yellow journalism, just without the journalism. He used the paper to extort and control high profile people, like public officials. In 1912, he targeted the mayor, Henry Schriver, with a story headlined: "Schriver's Shame! Spent Night and Day in Peoria in Filthy Debauch with Ethel: Deed that Would Shame a Dog!" The mayor was a bit steamed, so he ordered the newspaper closed and Looney arrested. Looney was not only arrested but beaten severely enough to require medical treatment. Looney's beating sparked two days of rioting that only ended when the Illinois governor declared martial law in Rock Island and sent in troops.

Shortly after this debacle, John Looney was tried in Peoria and convicted of mailing obscene material. He was fined $5,000 and ordered to cease publication of the *News*. Instead of reporting to prison, Looney slipped away to New Mexico. When he returned in 1917 he ramped up his efforts to control the city's vice, expanding his portfolio from the core business of gambling and prostitution to include bootlegging, thanks to Prohibition. A criminal empire of his magnitude requires considerable help, and so it was with Looney. People who were implicated in helping Looney included a former mayor, chief of police, and city attorney, plus most of the Rock Island Police Department.

In July 1922, Looney ordered the murder of tavern owner Bill Gabel, who was set to testify against

Wanted poster (courtesy of the Robert B. Wright family)

Looney in Federal court. Following Gabel's shooting, a gang war ensued in which 12 people died, culminating with an October attack on Looney himself in which his 22-year-old son was killed. After a crackdown by authorities, Looney was indicted for a variety of crimes, including the murder of Gable; he fled Rock Island in December 1922. Two years later he was captured in New Mexico and extradited to Illinois for trial. Convicted of murder, he served nine years in Joliet Prison before he was paroled. He died in 1947 at a tuberculosis sanitarium in El Paso, Texas.

In spite of this remarkable legacy, Rock Island never named anything after Looney.

(pronounced "boat-geez") is a small manufacturer of award-winning stone-ground mustard, using a recipe unchanged since *Fred Herman Boetje* made the first batch in the late 1880s. Tours include an overview of the mustard-making process, but, as they are a small operation, please call in advance to arrange a tour at a time that is convenient for them.

Sunset Park (Between 18th Ave. & 31st Ave.; 309.732.2000) is a good place to stop for a picnic and to take in some river views. In winter, I have spotted several bald eagles here.

Continue to downtown Rock Island, aka The District. Find a parking place and explore The District on foot. Park at one of the free spots on the street (two-hour limit) or go to the garage on 16th Street between 3rd Avenue and 4th Avenue and pay the astronomical sum of .25/hour (or nothing at all after 5 p.m. and on weekends).

The Centennial Bridge Visitors Center (201 15th St.; 309.277.0937; Th–Sa 10–6, Su 10–4) has the standard visitor center shtick like brochures plus displays about the construction of the Centennial Bridge and other Mississippi River bridges in the Quad Cities.

✔ TIP: If you think you might like to take a walking tour of the Augustana Campus, pick up a booklet here. You can also get a copy at the Rock Island Public Library.

MidCoast Fine Arts Left Bank Gallery (1629 2nd Ave.; 309.732.1354; Tu–Th,Sa 10–5 F 10–7; free) has a decent collection of work created by local artists for viewing or for purchase. **Quad Cities Arts** (1715 2nd Ave.; 309.793.1213; M,Tu,Th 10–5, W,F 10–9, Sa 10–6; free) is a more impressive gallery, however. Housed in the 1920s-era London Building, this is part gallery space and part retail space that shines the light on the work of local and regional artists. The quality is consistently high and you can find something in virtually any price range. If you are only going to visit one of these galleries, visit Quad Cities Arts.

How about one more arty place? If the garage door is open, which is more likely to happen early or late in the day during the summer, feel free to wander over and watch glass artist Mark Fowler at work at the **Liquid Fire Studio** (200 24th St.; 309.269.8668; no set schedule). As of this writing, the **Quad Cities Wood Turners** (2324 3rd Ave.) were renovating a building that will house several artists and possibly a gallery space. If you are interested in the art of wood turning, stop by the building and check out their progress.

✔ TIP: Although Liquid Fire Studio is not set up for retail, you can find some of his pieces for sale at Quad Cities Arts.

Quad City Botanical Center (2525 4th Ave.; 309.794.0991; M–Sa 10–5, Su 12–5; $5) offers quiet spaces to enjoy in its tropical house and small outdoor gardens.

Founded in 1860 in Chicago as Augustana College and Theological Seminary, **Augustana College** was affiliated with the Augustana Lutheran Synod, a national denomination composed primarily of Swedish immigrants and their families. The school moved to Paxton, Illinois before settling in Rock Island in 1875. The College now offers a full liberal arts curriculum, without the seminary, and maintains a relationship with the Evangelical Lutheran Church of America. The campus has a number of attractions that are fully described in a walking-tour brochure available around town. If

For more information and updates, visit my web site at www.mississippivalleytraveler.com.

you have limited time, the attractions described below won't disappoint. Parking around the college can be a challenge but lot E next to Centennial Hall (7th Ave. @ 38th St.) usually has spots for visitors. You may also be able to find a spot on 38th Street.

✔ **TIP: Many of the attractions on the Augustana campus have peak hours during the academic year, which is roughly from mid-August to mid-May. If you want to visit any of the campus sites discussed here and you are visiting in the summer, you should call ahead to verify their hours.**

The Augustana College Art Museum (Centennial Hall, 3703 7th Ave.; 309.794.7231; Open during the school year on W,F 1–4, Tu,Th–Sa 12–4, call for summer hours; free) houses an impressive collection of art in temporary exhibits in the upper and lower lobbies, as well as pieces from their permanent collection in a lower level gallery.

The Fryxell Geology Museum (Swenson Hall; 309.794.7318; M–F from 8–4:30, Sa,Su 1–4; summer hours M–F 9–1; closed mid-July to mid-August; free) may be modest in size, but it makes a big impression with its collection of fossils and rocks. The fossil of a Tylosaurus Proriger, a sixteen-foot-long eel-like reptile, will either impress or scare the heck out of you. Look for it on the rear wall. The back corner of the museum has a display showing off the fluorescent quality of several different minerals; pull the black curtain around you for a fun light show. The museum is in Swenson Hall on the heart of the campus, near the admissions office and the planetarium.

Have some more time? The **John Deere Planetarium** is next door (309.794.7327; 45-minute shows by appointment during the academic year, generally for groups only; free). Even if you can't take in a show, they have some cool meteor samples in the hallway. As you go back downhill, the doorway to your left under the arch (the entrance for the admissions office) has a gothic-inspired chapel on the second floor, **Ascension Chapel**.

✔ TIP: The City of Rock Island published a driving tour that highlights sights around town that were tied to its infamous mobster. You can download a copy of the John Looney Legend Tour (www.rigov.org/pdf/CED/ brochures/Looneytourbrochure.pdf), or you pick up a free copy at the Rock Island Public Library or City Hall. Many of the sites are now private residences and a few are parking lots, so you may want to be selective about the sites you visit. Some of the more notorious sites include Looney's Roost (2012 16th Avenue), the Looney mansion (1635 20th Street), and the house of his lawyer, Frank Kelly, across the street (1703 20th Street). Even if you opt to skip the tour, the brochure is an interesting read for the Looney history.

✔ BONUS TIP: The City of Rock Island published several other walking tours to the city's neighborhoods and architecture. Look for them at the library, city hall (2nd floor), or visitors' centers, or download a copy from www.rigov.org/visitors/walkingtour.html.

Entertainment ☼

COMEDY SPORTZ (1818 3rd Ave.; 309.786.7733; F, Sa 7p; $10 in advance, $12 at the door) performs improvisational comedy shows on weekends.

JUMER'S CASINO (Illinois Highway 92 @ Interstate 280; 800.477.7747/309.793.4200; daily 8a–3a) opened a new land-based facility in December 2008. The art deco-inspired casino has a spacious 42,000 square feet of gaming space, with over 1,100 slot machines and 24 gaming tables, plus a hotel and restaurants.

Live Music ♂

HUCKLEBERRY'S PIZZA & CALZONES (223 18th St., 309.786.1122) is a pizza joint by day (restaurant hours Tu–Th 11–9, F 11–11, Sa 4:30–11, Su 4:30–9) and occasional concert venue by night, hosting an impressive range of local bands and regional touring acts.

RIBCO (1815 2nd Ave.; 309.793.1999; M–F 11a–3a, Sa 5p–3a) has an extensive beer list and live music on weekends; the crowd generally skews toward the 20-something set.

Bars ♈

BLUE CAT BREWERY in Rock Island (113 18th St.; 309.788.8247; M–Sa 11a–3a, upstairs bar also open Su 9p–3a) has friendly regulars, quite possibly the best bartender in the entire Quad Cities, Bob, and me, when I'm in town. This is an easy place to pass the time drinking craft beers and chatting with friends. I've never been bored here. The upstairs bar has pool tables and bar games aplenty. (See also under "Food.")

If you are in a martini mood, head over to **ICON'S MARTINI BAR** (124 18th St.; 309.788.4266; T–Th 4p–1a, F,Sa 4p–3a), which tends to attract a more upscale-minded crowd.

For a more relaxed option, try **STEVE'S OLD TIME TAP BAR & GRILL** (223 17th St.; 309.786.4543; daily 11a–3a), an old-school neighborhood tavern that draws a cross section of Rock

For more information and updates, visit my web site at www.mississippivalleytraveler.com.

First Railroad Bridge Across the Mississippi

The Rock Island Bridge, the first railroad bridge across the Mississippi River, opened on April 22, 1856. The steamboat industry was not amused. The bridge, with eight fixed spans and one swing span, connected Davenport and Rock Island and appeared to have been built to deliberately interfere with steamboat traffic: the draw span was built at an angle to the current, making navigating under it exceptionally difficult.

Two weeks after the opening, the steamer *Effie Afton* proved the point when it crashed into the new bridge. All of the passengers were rescued, but the boat burned and sank, damaging the bridge in the process; the owners of the *Effie Afton* responded by suing the bridge company. Their case was heard in a Federal court in Chicago where one of the lawyers for the bridge company was Abraham Lincoln. The case worked its way to the U.S. Supreme Court, which ruled in favor of bridge interests in 1872. The ruling triggered a wave of new bridge construction across the Mississippi River.

The Rock Island Bridge was replaced by a new bridge in 1872, but not after causing steamboat pilots headaches for years. In 1857 alone, 50 steamboats ran into it. Part of an original bridge pier has been preserved and is visible on Arsenal Island near the Davenport House. The City of Davenport built a replica pier and threw on a commemorative plaque; it is located on the north side of River Drive at 4th Street, just east of the *Quad Cities Times*' offices.

Islanders.

AUGIES ON 20TH (313 20th St.; 309.788.7389; daily 3p–3a) has a corner-bar feel and a largely gay male clientele.

Accommodations 🏠

There is one campground in Rock Island. • **KOA ROCK ISLAND/QUAD CITIES** (2311 78th Ave. West; 800.787.0605/309.787.0665) is south of I-80 and east of Iowa Highway 92 and has 147 cramped sites ($16–$60) and eight cabins ($55–$73).

• **HOLIDAY INN ROCK ISLAND/QUAD CITIES** (226 17th St.; 888.465.4329/309.794.1212; $104–$265; WiFi) is a high-rise hotel in the heart of The District. There are two bed-and-breakfasts in Rock Island neighborhoods. • The **VICTORIAN INN** (702 20th St.; 800.728.7068/309.788.7068; $70–$90 + tax, incl full breakfast and WiFi) is a cozy bed-and-breakfast with beautiful Flemish tapestries in the dining room; it is located in the Broadway neighborhood. • **TOP O' THE MORNING** (1505 19th Ave.; 309.786.3513; $70–$140 + tax, incl full breakfast) is a bluff-top B&B in a prairie-style mansion built in 1912 as summer home for Hiram Cable, the one-time president of the Rock Island Railroad; they cater to married couples only.

Food 🍴

THEO'S JAVA CLUB (213 17th St.; 309.788.5282; M–Th 6a–10p, F 6a–midnight, Sa 8a–midnight) draws a diverse crowd for its coffee, snacks, soup ($2.30), sandwiches (about $4), and free WiFi. Bring cash; Theo's does not accept credit cards.

14TH AVENUE WAFFLE HOUSE (4128 14th

Confederate Cemetery on Arsenal Island

Ave.; 309.788.4181; M–Sa 5a–11a) is a traditional
mom-and-pop diner run by the same mom and pop
for 22 years. You can eat very well here for under $4 or
splurge on a steak and eggs for about $7.

MAMA COMPTON'S (1706 3rd Ave.;
309.786.6262; M–F 9–4, Sa 10–3) crafts salads and
sandwiches built with bread baked in-house (< $6).
On my first visit, I forgot to add a condiment to my
turkey sandwich, but the marble rye bread was so
flavorful and moist, I didn't miss the mayo. They also
have ice cream—very good ice cream.

Another local favorite for ice cream is **WHITEY'S**.
They have several stores around town. In Rock
Island, check out the store at 2520 18th Avenue
(309.788.5948, M-Th 10a-10p, F,Sa 10a-11p). A
single scoop costs about $2 and a regular shake about
$4.

BLUE CAT BREW PUB (113 18th St.;
309.788.8247; full menu served M–Sa 11a–11p, ap-
petizers served M–Th until midnight and F,Sa until 1
a.m.) has an extensive menu of affordable, consistently
pleasing comfort food-leaning favorites ($6–$17). I

adore the meatloaf and brisket.

JIM'S RIB HAVEN (531 24th St.; 309.786.8084; Tu–Th 11–10, F,Sa 11–11, Su Noon–9) serves up good, hearty barbecue dishes like sandwich platters ($8) and saucy rib platters (half rack for $14).

ATLANTE TRATTORIA (140 18th St.; 309.788.2805; M–W 8a–2p, Th,F 8a–2p, 5-8, Sa 5-8) is a great place to grab a freshly prepared, light meal at a reasonable price (sandwiches, soups, salads all generally less than $6).

LA RANCHARITA (4118 14th Ave.; 309.794.1648; M–Th,Su 8a–10p, F,Sa 8a–midnight) is another quality Mexican restaurant with good food, good prices (entrees $5–$10), and good service; it can be very busy on weekend evenings.

LE FIGARO FRENCH RESTAURANT (1708 2nd Ave.; 309.786.4944; Tu–Sa 5–10p but closed in July) serves French-inspired cuisine in a classy-casual setting (most entrees $14–$26 but specials run to $39). The entrees run the gamut of succulent meat-centered meals such as duck with orange or raspberry sauce, but they also offer a vegetarian entree. If you are in the mood for something lighter, the adjacent **STAR BAR** has a good selection of soups and salads ($3.50-$5), plus several delicious tapas dishes like bacon-wrapped dates, escargots, and mini Beef Wellington ($5–$8).

Resources

- Main Post Office: 2633 11th St.; 309.788.2142.
- Rock Island Public Library—Main: 401 19th St.; 309.732.7323; M–Th 9–9, F,Sa 9–5:30.

MOLINE, ILLINOIS

(population 43,768)

Arriving in Town

Welcome to Moline. After 44th Street, River Drive
will take you all the way through town.

Early History

Moline is another municipality that was founded on
land originally owned by *Antoine LeClaire*. He sold
several parcels to early settlers, many of whom were
migrants from New England. Among them was *David
Sears*, who built a dam between the mainland and
Rock Island in order to power a mill. It opened in
1838 and worked out so well that he built two more.
These early mills may have provided the inspiration for
the town's name, which the early leaders chose because
they believed it was derived from a French word for
"Milltown."

John Deere moved his primary factory to Moline
in 1848 because of the location's proximity to coal,
transportation, and a good supply of workers. Most
of the workers were new arrivals from Europe, including a substantial number of Swedes. The company
grew quickly, and its plows, and the John Deere name,
spread throughout the Midwest. One of his early partners was *John Gould*. Deere bought out Gould's interests within a few years but Gould went on to establish
a furniture factory, then a sawmill, before becoming a
bank president.

The railroads reached Moline in 1854. The following year, Moline re-incorporated with strict liquor laws

Map of Downtown Moline

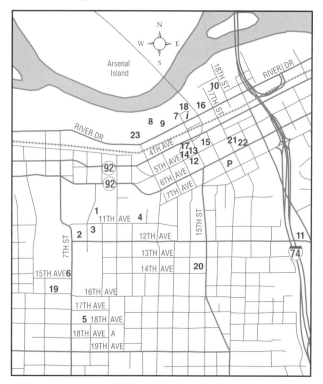

i - Moline Visitor Center
P - Parking
1. Deere-Wiman House
2. Butterworth Center
3. Rock Island County Historical
   Society
4. Velie Park
5. Center for Belgian Culture
6. Stephens Park
7. John Deere Commons
8. Spirit of Place
9. Radisson on John Deere
   Commons
10. Stoney Creek Inn

11. Economy Inn
12. Lagomarcinos
13. Thongsy's Thai Restaurant
14. Bent River Brewing Company
15. La Flama
16. River House Bar & Grill
17. Bier Stube
18. Bass Street Chop House
19. Belgian Village Inn
20. El Mariachi
21. Main Post Office
22. Moline Downtown Library
23. Moline Centre Station

and new powers to maintain the city's thoroughfares. The city required able-bodied males between 21 and 50 years old to work on road projects up to three days per year. Moline's early leaders, proud of their Puritan heritage, reportedly encouraged people with inferior values to settle elsewhere, like in Rock Island.

Moline's manufacturing base grew partly because of the reluctance of landowners in Rock Island to sell prime real estate. The factories that lined Moline's riverfront included workers of many European nationalities, including Swedes, Germans, Irish, and Belgians. The Belgian community grew into the second largest in the United States; for many years Moline was home to a Belgian consulate. With the exception of the Belgians, most factory workers actually lived in Davenport or Rock Island, not Moline.

In 1900 Moline had about 22,000 residents, 5,200 of whom worked in factories. Fully one-third of the factory workers worked at John Deere and another 1,200 at Moline Plow. No wonder Moline was nicknamed "Plow City" and "John Deere Town."

Attractions

Just to your left as you drive on 44th Street is the site of what was once another massive factory next to the river. International Harvester bought the factory from the Moline Plow Company in 1926 and renamed it Farmall Works. They produced millions of big red tractors until the factory was shuttered in 1986. Most of the old plant was demolished in 2008.

Who says America doesn't have any cool ruins? The atmospheric setting of **Sylvan Island** (1st Ave. @ 2nd St.; 309.736.5714; daily sunrise–sunset) was the site of the mammoth Republic Steel Works that operated from 1894 to 1956; all that remains is the concrete foundations that ornament the island with post-industrial ruins. If you are lucky, you will explore this place on a foggy, slightly cool day around dawn or dusk.

Take a side trip to explore a cluster of historic houses. The two most impressive houses are the **Deere-Wiman House** (817 11th Ave.; free) and the **Butterworth Center** (1105 8th St.; free) and they could not be more different. The Deere-Wiman house is an exceptional example of 19th century Victorian stylings, with gorgeous walnut paneling on the first floor, a music room complete with a pipe organ, and one of the earliest multiple head full-body showers. And you thought the Victorian era lacked sensuality. In contrast, the Butterworth Center feels like a medieval castle when you enter the foyer, an impression that is cemented after entering the stunning library. Like the Deere-Wiman House, the Butterworth Center has a pipe organ, but, then again, whose house doesn't? Both houses are open for guided tours on Sundays from 1–4 in July and August or by appointment the rest of the year (309.765.7971).

Across the street from the Deere-Wiman House is the **Rock Island County Historical Society** (822 11th Ave. 309.764.8590), which not only hosts an impressive genealogy and local history collection (open W-Sa 9-4) but also manages a house and a carriage museum (tours by appointment; free). The house itself is not nearly as impressive as the two Deere family houses (there are few original furnishings) but has interesting displays of local history, including replicas of 19th century dentist's and doctor's offices and an 1840s-era bedroom.

Nearby **Velie Park** (11th St. @ 11th Ave.) was named for *Willard Lamb Velie*, grandson of John Deere, and founder of the Velie Carriage Company. From 1908 to 1928 they produced 75,000 cars, but the company came to an abrupt end in 1929 when

What John Deere's Invention Changed

John Deere was born in Rutland, Vermont, on February 7, 1804. Trained as a blacksmith, he moved to Grand Detour, Illinois, in 1836 on the heels of bankruptcy. When Deere arrived in the Midwest, farmers were using the cast-iron plows that had been very effective in tilling the thinner, rockier soil on the East Coast. In the Midwest, however, the cast-iron plows were better at attracting dirt than tilling it; after just a few feet, the plow had to be cleaned of accumulated dirt, making plowing an arduous and nearly impractical job. At a time when many farmers were frustrated and ready to abandon farming in the Midwest, John Deere crafted a cast-steel plow that not only cut through the soil more quickly but was also self-cleaning. This simple invention, made initially from a saw blade, eased the task of tilling the tough Midwestern soil and opened up the prairies to farming.

The company has since grown well beyond plow-making and has survived a number of difficult economic times, including a brush with bankruptcy in 1857 and the difficult 1980s. It remains one of the largest employers in the Quad Cities and has kept its corporate headquarters in Moline.

Willard and his son died within a month of each other.
The park has a nice overlook of Moline and the Mississippi River.

✔ **TIP: If you want to see the last home of the original John Deere, head to the northeast corner of 12th Street and 11th Avenue. This is the only residence of his that has not been leveled.**

The Center for Belgian Culture (712 18th Ave.; 309.762.0167; W,Sa 1–4; free) is a storefront museum that has a small collection of exhibits about Belgian life in the Quad Cities, with displays about homing pigeons, lace, and a game called Rolle Bolle, which you can still play at Stephens Park (15th Ave. @ 7th St.). Stop by the Center on the first Saturday of the month for a genuine Belgian waffle breakfast (8a–noon; $5).

John Deere Commons (River Dr. @ 15th St.) is a megaplex of attractions honoring the John Deere legacy in Moline (see the side story on page 99). Parking is plentiful, with free surface lots on 15th Street behind the John Deere Pavilion or across the street in a much larger lot. A pay garage is a little further on 15th Street across the railroad tracks; it is free after 5 p.m. Street parking is free but limited to two hours. The Mid-Town Ramp (17th St. @ 6th Ave.) also has free two-hour parking.

At the **John Deere Pavilion** (1400 River Dr.; 309.765.1000; M–F 9–5, Sa 10–5, Su 12–4; free), climb into the cockpit of a giant 9970 Cotton Picker and get a new perspective on the world. A number of different models of tractors, combines, and other giant farm trucks are on display; you are encouraged to touch and climb into the seats of most of them, so I did. Next door to the pavilion is the **John Deere Store** (1300 River Dr.; 888.231.1236/309.765.1007; M–F 10–6, Sa 10–5, Su 12–4), where you can buy model

John Deere Pavilion, Moline, Illinois

tractors, T-shirts, hats and other memorabilia, all with
the John Deere logo, of course. Just across the street,
between the convention center and the Radisson Hotel, is the sculpture Spirit of Place that was installed to
mark and honor the site of the first John Deere factory
in Moline. If you have time to tour the **John Deere
Factory** in East Moline where they build the huge
combines, please do so. The 90-minute tour takes you
through the entire manufacturing process and is totally
awesome! I was so distracted by watching the production process that I missed half of what our guide said.
Guess I need to go back. The tour is free but you must
call in advance to make a reservation (800.765.9588/
877.201.3924). Tours are available Monday through
Friday at 8, 10, and 12:30. You can take still pictures
but not video, and don't even think of showing up in
open-toed shoes.

   John Deere World Headquarters (1 John Deere
Place; 800.765.9588/309.765.8000; daily 9–5; free).
Designed by noted architect *Eero Saarinen*, who also
designed that Arch thing in St. Louis, the HQ campus

for John Deere is the prototypical corporate suburban campus. Then-CEO *William Hewitt* wanted a building that fit the John Deere corporate image—modern but not flashy. How Midwestern! He got his wishes. The buildings are constructed of Cor-ten steel, a material previously developed for railroads that weathers as it ages, creating a rust-free barrier. Clever. Most buildings are private but the main building at the top of the hill has an exhibit hall that is open to the public where you can once again climb on farm equipment, watch videos, and read about the company's history. The trip from downtown Moline will only take about ten minutes.

✔ **TIP: If you still haven't had enough of John Deere, take a side trip to the location where it all began. The John Deere Historic Site (8393 S. Main, Grand Detour, Ill.; 815.652.4551; daily 9–5 from April 1–November 30; $3) is located in Grand Detour, near Dixon, Ill., a 90-minute drive from Moline. Guided tours lasting about 75 minutes will take you around the original homestead of John Deere where he invented the first self-cleaning plow. The tour includes a replica of John Deere's blacksmith shop.**

The **Niabi Zoo** (13010 Niabi Zoo Rd.; 309.799.5107; daily spring–Labor Day from 9:30–5, from Sep 2–Oct 26 open M–F 11–4, Sa,Su 9:30–5, from Oct 27–Dec 6 open Sa,Su 11–4; $5), located in Coal Valley, is a bit out of the way but has some fun exhibits for a small zoo. Especially entertaining is the Australian Walkabout, where you can strut alongside an emu or hold a lorikeet.

Live Music ☛

At **BENT RIVER BREWING COMPANY** (Moline: 1413 5th Ave.; 309.797.2722; M,W,Th 11a–2a, Tu,F,Sa 11a–3, Su 11a–1a; modest cover charge on weekends), every day is the summer of love and the food is groovy, too. Bent River has a large selection of handcrafted beer (the uncommon stout is my personal favorite), live music on weekends that leans toward rock and folk music, and a big patio that is more enjoyable in June than January. The service can be very laid back, so don't show up starving or dehydrated. (See also under "Food.")

Bars ♈

CHRISTOPHER D'S (514 16th St.; 309.764.9613; daily 11a–3a) is the kind of place you crave after a long shift at John Deere, a tavern where you can have a cold beer while watching the Cubs play. Friendly bartenders, lots of TVs, a grill open late (I love the Southwest Burger!), and a pool table—the kind of place one could get very comfortable.

On Saturday nights, **LA FLAMA** (1514 5th Ave.; 309.797.3756) morphs from Mexican restaurant to Salsa dance club. All are welcome, even me, when I danced salsa—poorly—with another man. Dancing begins at 10:30 p.m. and ends around 1:30 a.m.

Good German beer tastes even better when enjoyed in the beer garden at the **BIER STUBE** (417 15th St.; 309.797.3040; M–Th 11–10, F,Sa 11–11, Su 11–9).

Shopping 💳

In Moline Centre, • **ISABEL BLOOM** (1505 River Dr.; 309.797.4255; M–F 10-6, Sa 10–5, Su 12–4), crafters of cast concrete sculptures, has another retail store. • **THE JOHN DEERE STORE** (1300 River Dr.; 888.231.1236/309.765.1007; M–F 10–6, Sa 10–5, Su Noon–4) sells, well, all things related to or carrying the logo of the famous company. • **BAKER STREET** (1601 River Dr., Suite 104; 309.762.9267; M–F 9-8, Sa 10–8, Su Noon–4) is your source for premium cigars. • **WATERMARK CORNERS** (1500 River Dr.; 309.764.0055; M–F 10–6, Sa 10–5) has an eclectic mix of greeting cards, gourmet food products, and home furnishings.

• **SOUTHPARK MALL** is near the airport in southern Moline (4500 16th St.; 309.797.9070; M–Sa 10–9, Su Noon–6).

Accommodations ⌂

There are three properties along the Moline Riverfront. In Moline Centre, the upscale • **RADISSON** on John Deere Commons (1415 River Dr.; 888.201.1 718/309.764.1000; $134–$159; WiFi) has luxurious beds, and the • **STONEY CREEK INN** (101 18th St.; 800.659.2220/309.743.0101; $85–$105) has cozy rooms with a lodge-inspired décor. Less than a mile from downtown, the • **ECONOMY INN** (1191 19th St.; 309.764.9644; WiFi) offers midrange prices ($60 for 1 bed, $70 for two beds, $120 for a room with a whirlpool) for its spacious, clean rooms. • Moline has a number of chain motels concentrated around the Quad City Airport at I-74 and Illinois Highway 6, a quick five-minute drive from downtown Moline.

Another great option is the • **RIVEREDGE BED & BREAKFAST** (4234 River Dr.; 309.797.6442), which is on the Mississippi east of downtown. The two bedroom executive suite ($129 + tax Su-Th, $159 + tax F,Sa for up to two people, $10/person for each additional guest; incl continental breakfast and WiFi) is stocked with extras such as a full kitchen, spacious living room, separate entry, swimming pool, and great views of the river. If that's not enough, guests receive

For more information and updates, visit my web site at www.mississippivalleytraveler.com.

a complimentary bottle of wine at check-in. You will need to reserve well in advance for summer stays.

Food ✗

In 2008, **LAGOMARCINOS** (1422 5th Ave.; 309.764.1814; M–Sa 9–5:30) celebrated 100 years of making life in the Quad Cities a little sweeter. The quintessential soda fountain, they still make sodas with phosphate, but ice cream is their forte. Try a hot fudge sundae and languorously pour the fudge from its own fudge boat onto your ice cream.

THONGSY'S THAI RESTAURANT (1419 5th Ave.; 309.797.5855; M–Th 11–2,5–9, F11–2,5–10, Sa 5–10) serves a range of good Thai dishes at reasonable prices (most dinner entrees $7–$10, lunch specials about $5).

BENT RIVER BREWING COMPANY (1413 5th Ave.; 309.797.2722; kitchen open M–Sa 11a–10p, Su 11a–9p) is a brewpub that serves fairly standard bar food, but with some surprising twists like the linguine with tomatillo sauce (salads $5, sandwiches $6.50, entrees $12).

LA FLAMA (1514 5th Ave.; 309.797.3756; Tu–Th 11a–9p, F 11a–10p, Sa Noon–10p, Su Noon–8) serves a range of authentic Mexican dishes, including some surprises, like beef tongue. Most entrees are between $8 and $10, but you can eat cheaper than that, too. Deliciosa!

RIVER HOUSE BAR & GRILL (1510 River Dr.; 309.797.1234; M–Th 11–10, F,Sa 11–11, Su 11–8) is a popular eatery in downtown Moline housed in a historic building, complete with belt-operated ceiling fans. They have a large and varied menu and equally large serving sizes (entrees $8–$16).

The first time I walked into the **BIER STUBE** (417 15th St.; 309.797.3040; M–Th 11–10, F,Sa 11–11, Su 11–9), the dining room was packed full of people singing German drinking songs. I assumed that sort of thing must happen all the time here, but, alas, it is not so. I just happened to visit the restaurant at the same time as a large group of tourists from Germany. As you might guess, they have a German theme going here, with very good German food (entrees $7–$13.50) and an extensive collection of German beer and wine. Guten Apetit!

BASS STREET CHOP HOUSE (1601 River Dr.; 309.762.4700; M–Sa 5p–10p, Su 5p–9p) is a highly regarded steakhouse (salads $4–$19; entrees $20–$53; sides $5–$10); reservations are recommended.

You won't mistake **MAID RITE** (4100 4th Ave.; 309.797.4424; M,F,Sa 7a–9p, Tu–Th,Su 7a–4p) for a high-end steakhouse. It is a regional favorite that specializes in seasoned ground beef on a bun, kinda like a sloppy joe, except without the sauce (about $3). Get one with everything, including ketchup.

BELGIAN VILLAGE INN (560 17th Ave.; 309.764.9222; M–Th 11a–10p, F,Sa 11–11) serves huge, inexpensive sandwiches (whole sandwiches $6–$7, half sandwiches about $4.50; other entrees $10–$15) in a neighborhood tavern. They are best known for their reuben sandwiches; try one with raisin bread. Seriously. Bread, soups and desserts are made fresh daily. Skip the house salad, unless you are madly in love with iceberg lettuce.

EL MARIACHI (1317 15th St.; 309.797.3178; Tu–F 11–9, Sa 9–9, Su 9–8) is the real deal in Mexican food (entrees $6–$12). The Saturday buffet of authentic Mexican dishes is a good deal (11a–2p; $8).

EXOTIC THAI (3922 38th Ave.; 309.797.9998; M–F 11–3,5–10, Sa,Su 11–10), like its Davenport counterpart, is a bit out of the way, but worth the trip. They serve very good Thai dishes (entrees $8–$15) in an attractive setting.

Resources

- Main Post Office: 514 17th St.; 309.764.5011.
- Moline Downtown Library: 504 17th St.; 309.762.6883; M–Th 9–5:30, Sa 9–5.

EAST MOLINE, ILLINOIS

(population 20,333)

Arriving in Town

East Moline's River Road starts as 12th Avenue, which turns into 13th Avenue, then 13th Street, and finally Illinois Highway 84.

Early History

Two villages pre-dated East Moline. Watertown was platted in the 1850s but had grown little 20 years later. Nearby Happy Hollow sprang to life as a mining boom town. At its peak, 1,000 coal miners lived in unpainted, temporary homes next to the mines; they worked hard, fought plenty, and lived squarely in the midst of poverty. When the mines closed in the 1880s, the village emptied.

By the time East Moline was platted in 1895, these early villages had vanished and the land was mostly undeveloped swamp. The only signs of "civilization" were a single railroad shack and one house. Rock Islander *E.H. Guyer* had previously purchased options on the land and was ready to begin a massive public relations campaign to sell land to fulfill his dream of creating an industrial powerhouse of a city. The initial attempt to auction off plots of land, however, was a miserable failure and would have killed the whole venture except for the generosity of two men, *Jeremiah Keator* and *Charles Deere*, who stepped forward with enough cash to keep the effort alive. Revitalized, Guyer moved on with his plans and slowly started to attract business and residents. In the early years, East Moline succeeded in attracting industry but housing construction lagged behind. The opening of the Rock Island Railroad yard in neighboring Silvis only exacerbated the housing shortage; it would take several years for East Moline to build enough housing to satisfy demand.

Attractions

As you enter East Moline on 12th Ave., the big empty lot you pass on the left is another abandoned industrial site; the Case/International Harvester/New Holland factory that was on this site was razed in 2007. Just to your right is the business district, which spans 7th Street to 11th Street along 15th Avenue. This strip has a mix of ethnic stores, including Mexican grocers, Asian grocers, and an African market, plus a couple of Mexican restaurants.

At the point where 13th Avenue makes a sharp turn to the right, the giant factory on the left is the **John Deere Harvester Works**—the factory that builds combines and, unlike its competitors, is still going strong. If you have been paying attention, you will have just read about the John Deere factory tour that is way cool. See the Moline section for more detail.

There are few other attractions for travelers in East Moline, but, if you want an excuse to see something, stop at **Campbell's Island State Historic Site** (Island Ave.; 309.788.0177; daily sunrise–sunset; free). It was built to commemorate a skirmish on July 19, 1814, during the War of 1812, in which 16 people were killed by a group of British allied Sauk and Mesquakie Indians led by Black Hawk. Campbell's Island has long been a favorite recreation spot for area residents (it still has a marina) and is currently home for many river rats. The monument is nothing special but the views of the river are good and you will probably have the place to yourself.

Food ✗

FRIEDA'S EUROPEAN BAKERY AND TEA ROOM (561 17th Ave.; 309.751.9570; Tu–Sa 7:30–2:30) is best loved for their tortes and pies ($3.25 for a slice), but they also offer good breakfast options (most items under $6), sandwiches ($4–$7), and German-influenced lunch platters ($7–$13).

THE HUNGRY HOBO is a popular local sandwich purveyor, with bread and soup made fresh daily. They have several stores around the area; in East Moline, the store closest to the River Road is on East Locust at Bridge Avenue (1842 18th Ave..; 309.755.9123; M–Sa 10-9, Su 11-9).

Resources

• Main Post Office: 805 16th Ave.; 309.755.5746.

• East Moline Public Library: 740 16th Ave.; 309.755.9614; M,W 9–8, Tu,Th 9–5, Sa 9–4 from Memorial Day–Labor Day, M–Th 9–9, F 9–5, Sa 9–4 the rest of the year.

HAMPTON, ILLINOIS

(population 1,626)

Arriving in Town

Illinois Highway 84 skirts the eastern edge of town. First Avenue is more or less the main drag and runs along the river.

History

Henry McNeal, born in Canada in 1811, left home at a very young age and went west. He worked on the Great Lakes and in the lead mines of Galena for a while. In 1828, at the ripe old age of 17, he moved farther south and built a log cabin next to the Mississippi River. A small community grew up around him that became known, appropriately enough, as McNeal's Landing.

The villages of Milan (not the current one but the one that was first called Well's Ferry) and Hampton, which included the older settlement of McNeal's Landing, were platted in 1837 and 1838 and both villages grew quickly. Hampton was a steamboat stop and had two hotels by the late 1830s and a horse-powered Mississippi River ferry. The town seemed destined for prosperity, perhaps even greatness. Alas, 19th century political chicanery put a halt to its rapid growth.

In 1833, Hampton and rival Farnhamsburg (now Rock Island) competed for the coveted county seat. The men of Farnhamsburg had already decided that their town would get the courthouse, they just needed to find a way to ensure that the vote confirmed their decision. They enlisted the help of *Colonel Davenport* to signal island voters, should their votes be needed to swing the election. When Davenport waved his hand-kerchief in signal, the Hampton men saw the move and were ready. Knowing the outcome had been fixed, they seized the poll book and raced away. This would

Brettun and Black Mercantile and Historical Museum in Hampton, Illinois

ordinarily prevent any further votes from being cast. Ah, but the men of Hampton had been outwitted again. The Farnhamsburg voters had antici-pated Hampton's move and replaced the real poll book with one that was blank. When the Hamptoners were safely out of sight, they retrieved the real book and continued voting. Farnhamsburg won the county seat and Hampton was consigned to the life of a quiet river town.

Attractions

Located in Hampton River Park adjacent to Empire Park, **the Hampton Heritage Center** (309.755.8398; M,W,F 9–1, Tu,Th 1–5; free) is primarily an event center, but if you are in the neighborhood when it is open, stop in to see the gigantic sculpted Gingko tree. When it became obvious that the large beloved tree was dying, artist *Thom Gleich* was commissioned to turn it into art, which he did by sculpting multiple images that explore the history of the region. If you stopped at Credit Island, you saw another sample of his work—the life-size sculptures from Seurat's paint-ing, A Sunday on La Grande Jette.

The Brettun & Black Mercantile and Historical Museum (601 First Ave.; 309.755.6265; Sa,Su 2–5;

free) is housed in a former store, built in 1849, that served as a critical source of supplies for residents of the northwest Illinois frontier. The museum has displays about local history and a faithfully restored version of the store proper, where you can still spend your dollars on items such as bread and butter pickles, homemade apple butter, or a bonnet.

The Illiniwek Forest Preserve (309.496.2620; daily sunrise–sunset) has several unmarked hiking trails and an overlook, which is a five- to ten-minute hike up a steep slope. If you want a little longer hike, turn right at the fork in the trail at the top of the hill, then take every left turn until you get to the overlook, a total of about 20 minutes of hiking up and down several hills. Bring bug spray. I didn't. I got chewed up.

Resources
- Post Office: 625 8th St.; 309.496.3300.

Accommodations ♠

The area around Hampton has two campgrounds.
• **FISHERMAN'S CORNER RECREATION AREA** (16123 State Highway 84 North; 877.444.6777/309.496.2720) has 51 sites with electricity and five primitive sites ($10–$18). • **ILLINIWEK FOREST PRESERVE** (Illinois Highway 84; 309.496.2620) has 60 sites with electricity and 25 basic sites ($11–$14).

Food ✗

THE RIVER ROAD RESTAURANT (421 State Ave.; 309.755.9230; Su–Th 6a–9p, F,Sa 6a–10p) has an extensive menu of breakfast foods ($5–$7), sandwiches and salads ($6–$7), and entrees ($7–$15), plus a few Greek standards like spanikopita, gyros, and baklava.

REGIONAL INFORMATION

When to Go

Now! What are you waiting for? Seriously, the Quad Cities will entertain you any time of year, although it can be a bit hot in the summer and a bit chilly in the winter. Average highs range from 30° F in January to 85° F in July, but the weather can be just a bit variable. In 1936, the Quad Cities endured a winter marked by three consecutive weeks of subzero temperatures, then suffered through a summer that brought record heat, including eleven straight days above 100° F and the single-day record high temperature (111° F). Welcome to the Midwest.

Winter is prime time for eagle watching. If you are into winter sports like ice skating and shoveling snow, this is your time of year. In spring, the snow melts, thunderstorms roll in, the rivers flood, and birds migrate north. Summer is the time to get out your boat, go fishing or waterskiing, and swat mosquitoes. In fall, the leaves turn color, the temperatures cool down, birds return south, and residents prepare their dens for winter.

Festivals

The Quad Cities are festival crazy. Something is happening most every time of year, especially in the summer when it seems there is a festival every weekend. Here are some of the most entertaining.

Celtic Games Bagpipe Band

Winter

Bald Eagle Days (Rock Island: QCCA Expo Center, 2621 4th Ave.; 309.794.5338; $4; January, 2nd weekend) in the Quad Cities is part exposition and part eagle watching. The exposition hall has conservation exhibits, animal shows, art, and Native American storytelling and dancing.

The Mississippi River Visitors' Center (Arsenal Island: 309.794.5338; Sa,Su 9:30, 11a, 1p; free) hosts a **Bald Eagle Watch** on the first few weekends of the new year except the weekend of Bald Eagle Days. The hour-long event includes a presentation on eagle biology, a tour of the Clock Tower, and eagle spotting. Reservations are required.

Spring

The **St. Patrick's Day Grand Parade** begins in Rock Island and crosses into Davenport via the Centennial Bridge, thus giving the Quad Cities bragging rights as host of the only St. Patrick's Day Parade that marches in two states, and, I imagine, that crosses a big river in the process (Davenport and Rock Island:

309.324.5000; March, generally the Saturday before St. Patrick's Day).

Motorcycle enthusiasts gather in Davenport on Father's Day weekend for **Sturgis on the River** (Davenport: 309.799.7469) to celebrate all things bike-ish with music, shopping, and ultimate fighting.

Summer

Mississippi Valley Blues Festival (Davenport's LeClaire Park; 563.322.5837; late June or early July) is a big blues bash on the Davenport riverfront. The festival draws top quality regional and national blues performers and big crowds.

Mississippi Valley Fair (Davenport: Mississippi Valley Fairgrounds; 2815 W. Locust; 563.326.5338; late July/early August) is a traditional county fair with traditional fair food like deep-fried mutant chicken breasts on a stick and traditional fair events like trying not to step in fresh cow dung.

The most well-known and best-attended festival is the **Bix Beiderbecke Memorial Jazz Festival** (Davenport: July/last weekend), named after the renowned cornet player and jazz composer whose legend continued beyond his untimely death at age 28 (see side story on page 118). The event began in 1971 when musicians from the Bix Beiderbecke Memorial Jazz Band of New Jersey came to Davenport to play on the fortieth anniversary of his death. When word leaked out that the group was going to jam at the Holiday Inn, 2,000 people showed up. Thinking that this was a sign of continuing interest in the legacy of Bix, an annual festival was created. Good thinking. Concerts take place

Antique Flat Track Motorcycle Races, Davenport, Iowa

in several locations around town including LeClaire Park on the Davenport riverfront.

River Roots Live (Davenport: August/weekend before Labor Day), also at LeClaire Park, is a two-day celebration of the roots music of the Mississippi River valley. Held in conjunction with RibFest, you can relish the sounds while inhaling the smells and flavors of barbecued ribs. Proceeds from the festival benefit the River Music Experience.

Men in skirts, whirling and twirling about, cradling large heavy objects, grunting and screaming, throwing the objects as far as they can. What is this thing? No, silly, it is not some strange S/M ballet, although it may look like that at times. This is the **Celtic Highland Games of the Quad Cities** (Davenport: Mississippi Valley Fairgrounds; 2815 W. Locust; 309.794.0449; August/weekend before Labor Day), an annual event where men in kilts gather at the Mississippi Valley Fairgrounds in Davenport to compete in games imported from Celtic homelands, like the hammer throw, sheaf toss, and caber toss, all to the background accompaniment of roaming bagpipers.

Bix Beiderbecke

Bix Biederbecke (courtesy of Davenport Public Library)

Leon (Bix) Beiderbecke, born in 1903 in Davenport, taught himself to play the cornet and piano without ever learning to read sheet music. During his childhood, he would sneak down to the riverfront to listen to music on the boats. When he failed high school, his parents sent him to a boarding school near Chicago. His academics didn't improve but his music skills did, helped along by easy access to the speakeasies and their resident musicians. He stayed out late, playing music and drinking, which inevitably led to an early exit from school.

By age twenty, he was playing professionally with well-known musicians such as the Jean Goldkette Band. His fame grew in 1927 when he and saxophonist Frankie Trumbauer joined the Paul Whiteman Orchestra, then the best-known and best-paying outfit in the country. He developed a unique style, drawing influences from well-known New Orleans cornetists and from contemporary classical composers such as Stravinsky, Dubussy, and Ravel, but forging it into a style that was his alone. Louis Armstrong reportedly said of his music "Lots of cats tried to play like Bix; ain't none of them play like him yet."

Bix suffered from poor health during much of his life, and his lifestyle didn't help. He died on August 6, 1931, in a rented room in Manhattan, ostensibly from pneumonia, but a seizure brought on by delirium tremens was a likely factor, as well. He was just 28 years old.

The **Antique Flattrack Motorcycles Races** (Davenport: Mississippi Valley Fairgrounds; 2815 W. Locust; 515.966.9338; August/last Friday of the month) are a throwback to an earlier era. Antique bikes and some antique riders—there is at least one guy in his 80s who competes most years—race around a half-mile dirt track. I was prepared to be bored, but between the roar of the bikes, the potential for bloody wrecks from slipping on the dirt track, and the photo finishes, I found the whole thing pretty damned exciting! And, I didn't feel the least bit out of place surrounded by a sea of middle-aged, bearded, leather-clad biker-types, except when the guy behind me kept naming off the year and make of every single bike and all I could see was that it had two wheels.

If you are into fast cars, albeit small ones, the **Rock Island Grand Prix** (Labor Day weekend) is your event. Professional kart drivers (as in go-karts) from near and far zip around the streets of downtown Rock Island for a $25,000 prize. This race is a springboard to NASCAR for many drivers. Seriously.

Culture and the Arts

Besides the cultural institutions highlighted along the River Road, there are several others that are worth checking out. **The Catich Gallery** (Davenport: Galvin Fine Arts & Communications Center; 518 W. Locust St.; 563.333.6000; during the school year open Tu–F 1–5, by appt. during the summer) is a small visual arts gallery at St. Ambrose University that hosts rotating exhibits. **The Quad Cities Symphony Orchestra** (563.322.0931) performs several concerts a year at the Adler Theater in Davenport and Centennial Hall in Rock Island.

The Quad Cities have several active theater companies. Your best bet is to consult the arts calendar in the *River Cities' Reader*, but the following venues have regular events. The **Circa '21 Dinner Playhouse** (Rock Island: 1828 3rd Ave.; 309.786.7733; $35–$40) is a dinner theater with a very busy performance schedule throughout the year. The **Green Room Theater** (Rock Island: 1611 2nd Ave.; 309.786.5660) is a newcomer to the scene that stages a few shows during the year plus other live arts events. The **Quad City Music Guild** (309.762.6610; summer shows performed Th–Sa 7:30, Su 2p; $15) has been staging musical and dance entertainment in Moline's Prospect Park Auditorium (16th St. @ 30th Ave.) for over half a century. Call or check their web site for a current schedule. Because of limited parking, the Guild operates a shuttle service from South Park Mall (the southeast lot near JCPenney and Denny's Restaurant) to the auditorium for performances. **It's a Mystery!** (563.355.6100; $35) specializes in original comedy/mystery shows that invite audience participation; they perform a few times a year in the Quad Cities.

The art deco **Adler Theatre** (136 E. 3rd St., Davenport; 563.326.8500) is a performing-arts center that opened in 1931; renovated in the 1980s, it hosts live concerts, musical theater, as well as performances for the Ballet Quad Cities (309.786.3779; $20-$43) and Opera Quad Cities (563.355.7737). For other arts events, don't forget to check the calendar for the **Galvin Fine Arts Center** at St. Ambrose University (518 W. Locust St., Davenport; 563.333.6251) and **Centennial Hall** at Augustana College (Rock Island: 3703 7th Ave.; 309.794.7233).

✔ TIP: Grab a copy of the free *River Cities' Reader*, the independent weekly newspaper, or check out the events calendar in the *Quad City Times* for a rundown of the current events scene.

In the flood of June 2008, floodwaters nearly surrounded Woodmen's Field in Davenport, Iowa, but ballgames continued.

Sports and Recreation

The QC has a range of professional sports teams to get your adrenaline pumping. The **Quad Cities River Bandits** (Davenport: Modern Woodmen Park; 209 S. Gaines St.; 563.322.6348; $5–$9; April–September), a Class A minor league baseball team affiliated with the St. Louis Cardinals, play in one of the most scenic spots for a baseball game—anywhere—at a historic stadium on the Davenport riverfront.

Quad City Steam Wheelers (Moline: i Wireless Center; 1201 River Dr.; 309.797.8500; $10–$50; games from March–July) play arena football, a frantic indoor version of the sport that will keep your attention. **The Quad City Flames** (Moline: i Wireless Center; 1201 River Dr.; 309.764.7825; $8–$14; games played from October–March) play in the American Hockey League as an affiliate of the Calgary Flames. The **Quad Cities Riverhawks** (Moline: Wharton Field House; 1800 20th St.; 866.694.5728; $10; games from January–March) is a professional basketball team in the Premier Basketball League that plays in an atmospheric arena built in 1928.

Craving a swim? There are several outdoor pools and waterparks in the area waiting for you: **Whitewater Junction** (Rock Island: Longview Park, 18th Ave. @ 17th St.; 309.732.7946; M–F 11–8, Sa,Su 10–6; $7) and **Riverside Aquatic Center** (Moline: Riverside Park, 3300 5th Ave.; 309.797.0788; M–Th 11–6, F-Su 11–5 from June to mid-August; $7) both have a range of slides and water features for adults and children. **Ferjervary Park** (Davenport: 1900 Telegraph Rd.; 563.326.7829; $4; call to confirm times for open swim), near the Putnam Museum, has a large pool and water slides. In Bettendorf, **Splash Landing Aquatic Center** (Middle Park; 2220 23rd St.; 563.344.4124; M–F 11:30–5, Sa,Su 11:30–6; $5) has a pool with waterslides.

Fishing is a popular way to pass the time, although if you are serious about catching something worthwhile, your best bet is around the locks and dams. Don't forget to buy a fishing license. Iowa charges non-resident adults $9 for a one-day license or $16 for a three-day license. In Illinois, a 24-hour license costs $5.50 or you can buy a ten-day non-resident license for $13. You can purchase an Iowa fishing license online (https://www3.wildlifelicense.com/ia/start.php) or at several locations around town, including **Credit Island Bait Shop** (Davenport: 2304 W. River Dr.; 563.326.3370; daily 6:30a–7:30p) and **B&B Shooting Supplies** (Bettendorf: 2152 State St.; 563.355.4867; M–F 8–6, Sa 8–5). Illinois licenses can also be purchased on-line (https://www4.wildlifelicense.com/il/start.php) or in town at **Croegaerts Great Outdoors** (Rock Island: 4002 11th St.; 309.788.4868; M–F 7–7, Sa 6–5, Su 6–4) or **Porter's Village Rx** (Hampton: 621 State Ave.; 309.755.3862; daily 5a–11p in summer), which is part gas station convenience store, part pharmacy, and part bait shop.

Getting on the River

It is easier to get near the river than on the river in the Quad Cities. There are no places to rent a boat in the immediate area, but you do have a few other ways to experience the Mississippi River directly. The best way to get up close and personal with the river is by riding the **Channel Cat Water Taxis** (details below under Getting Around). For $6 you can ride all day; they even have room for a few bicycles. If you do a complete loop, the ride will take about an hour.

Another option is taking a ride on the **Celebration Belle** (2501 River Dr., Moline; 800.297.0034/309. 764.1952; standard cruise prices $12–$42; specialty cruises $50–$62; all-day cruises $141), which offers a variety of your standard tourist-oriented river cruises from Tuesday through Saturday, some with food, some without. Sightseeing cruises usually stick to the ten-mile stretch between the locks. The lunch cruise atmosphere was way too cheesy for my tastes, but the food was much better than I expected.

Local Media

Newspapers

- *Quad-City Times*
- *River Cities' Reader* (free independent weekly)
- *Rock Island Argus and The Dispatch*

Public Radio Station

- 90.3, WVIK; some NPR shows, but air time dominated by classical music.

For more information and updates, visit my web site at www.mississippivalleytraveler.com.

INDEX

S

T-U-V

W-X-Y-Z